MY NAME IS VERNE

HIS NAME WAS CLAY

A LOVE STORY
BY VERNON STUMP

"My Name is Verne, His Name was Clay, A Love Story"
ISBN-13: 978-0-578-53307-0
ISBN-10: 0-578-53307-3

Published by Clayver Publishing
Portsmouth, NH 03801

Special thanks in the production of this book to

Crystal Ward Kent, Kent Creative,
Editorial & Art Direction

Denise Brown, Ad-cetera Graphics,
Layout & Production

Budd Perry, Memories Studios,
Author photos, p. 124 and p. 127

Cover illustrations by Vernon Stump

Dedication:
To all who have known love

INTRODUCTION

This is a story about two people born in the mid-Twentieth Century, in two different parts of the country, and into two completely different environments. One was raised from birth by a loving family who gave him not only love but respect (and even adoration from some). The other was raised by two very headstrong women and had to fight for any love that might be found.

Both were raised in small towns and born into middle class families; these families were upwardly mobile and proud but there the similarities ended. One boy was taught to work hard and study hard. He believed that after completing higher education, he would be ready for a happy and successful life. The other boy was praised by one strong woman, but told by the other that whatever you got in life, you had to fight for — nothing was handed to you on a silver platter. One boy was very secure and loved, the other very insecure and scared.

Both ran afoul of the law in their early twenties — not because of who they were, but because of what society perceived them to be. One got married to prove to all that life was normal, while the other stayed single and tried to live his true life in the shadows.

Early in their first year together, a near tragic event made them take an unvoiced pledge of "until death do us part." Through their many years together, this pledge was never doubted, although for the first 25 years, one partner needed to be assured over and over that love was there and that he deserved it. It is a testament to the other partner that he was always ready to prove it. One would push away and the other would pull back. It wasn't a game — it was a battle that they both waged to overcome the great insecurity and fear buried deep in one partner's soul. It took years for him to finally let love happen.

In their last 30 years, good things happened in their relationship. A son from the marriage came back into their lives along with grandchildren and yes, even great-grandchildren. They went to Alaska to witness the marriage of a granddaughter. Finally, they achieved a normal life in a society that at last accepted them as normal. Most important, they were happy with themselves in their own lives.

In their last years together, one partner became very sick. After awhile, he got tired of being sick and quietly took his leave from this life. His passing came with a smile on his face and with his being surrounded by family, friends and the one he loved. "I love you," they said, and it was enough.

Clay, as I write this book, and ponder our life together, my question now is, "In death did we part or in death do we live?" I hope I see you again.

I love you, Clay.
— Your Verne

Clay at 24

Clay at 74

Clay and Verne in Costa Rica

CHAPTER ONE:
MY CLAY

If somebody were to ask me to describe my Clay I would have to say that he was many things to many people. He was very proud to be a Wilcox and pleased that he looked very much like his father. He wasn't tall and he wasn't short; he was 5' 7" but slightly built. When we first met, he had beautiful dark wavy hair that fell down over his ears and a dark mustache and beard. His dark eyes always seemed to twinkle and were very kind.

I learned that the smile was always just below the surface and came easily. His voice was soft and mellow, as was his singing voice, and he loved to sing—especially while cooking. His dress was casual but conservative and his shoes were always shined. One of the things I first noticed about him was that I could make him laugh—followed by the fact that he had a great sports car and a prestigious, respectable job.

Soon after meeting him, I found that he loved to cook and to dine out. He always enjoyed a 5:00 cocktail and smoked weed when I could get it for him. Most surprising—and appealing— he treated me like I had always dreamed of being treated.

Clay was the man of my mother's dreams and I was going to make him mine. After a few months of dinner, drinks and concerts, he finally asked me to spend the night with him. Even though he didn't meet my sexual fantasy, everything else about the relationship seemed too good to be true. After that first night together, we spent every one either at my place or his, and frequently, in the evening, he would play his guitar and sing to me. We held hands while driving and talked endlessly. After a few weeks, he asked me if we were lovers and I said, "Yes Clay, I think we are," and he smiled.

There were few things, or people, that Clay disliked. He didn't care for my brother-in-law but tolerated him, and he disliked tuna and sushi. He hated gossip and refused to take part in it. Other than that, he enjoyed almost anything.

His great loves, besides me, were his church, his singing, good music, cooking and being able to help people in need of counseling. He loved to read and could be found reading no matter the location — in the car, on the bed, on the toilet, or in his favorite spot, his rocker.

For all of his accomplishments, Clay was somewhat shy and very reserved. However, between the two of us, at parties, we managed to work a crowd well, and with just eye contact, we knew when it was time to leave.

Clay never talked much about his early life but often said that he had to do a lot of work on the farm, and so never had much time for after school activities like other kids. Because he had never shown any interest in girls, by the time he reached his teens his parents understood that he was gay. This did not seem to be an issue with them. In fact, the first time I visited Clay's family at their home, his father sat me down and confided that he had always worried about his favorite son because he was gay — he was afraid of what might happen to him. However, after meeting me, and seeing how much I loved Clay, he felt he did not have to worry any more.

The rest of the family was, initially, not as accepting. His younger brother, Jeff, said that he often had to fight battles at school because his classmates said that he had a "queer" brother. This resentment lingered for decades. When we lived in Boston, Jeff lived fairly near, but we never saw him. Nora, Clay's sister and dear friend, said that Jeff said that he would kill me if we ever met — that's how much he hated Clay's lifestyle. However, as time passed, Jeff changed and once we moved to Portsmouth, he and his family came to visit. Jeff and I now talk often and are fairly close. Clay's older brother, Jim, also resented him but for different reasons. Clay's mother had recognized Clay's academic ability early on and so gave him fewer chores to allow him to study, which left Jim to pick up the extra work. It was understandable that Jim would be angry, but it was not Clay's fault. We later visited Jim and his large family just once, when we lived in Eau Claire and he lived in Chicago, so some peace was made.

Clay was never interested in sports but loved Scottish dancing and contra dancing. He was involved in a number of groups, had taken lessons, and pursued it until his arthritis prevented him from doing so. He also sang in the church choir until the end.

In later years, when he began to suffer from the effects of age and ill health, we had an unspoken agreement that if he wanted help, he would ask for it, even when it came to walking. If he was feeling a little unstable, he would take my arm, smile his little smile, and always say, "Thanks, love!"

One thing that was unique in our relationship was that he never told me "no," even though I'm sure that there were many times he wanted to, and even though my headlong pursuit of certain things sometimes led to disaster. He would give advice and offer his opinion as to why I should or should not make a certain choice, but he never said "no."

At the start of our relationship, I told him never to say he loved me or it would be over, and he took me at my word, even although I sensed that he yearned to say it. It wasn't until we moved to Portsmouth, after being together for 37 years, that he asked if he could tell me he loved me. I finally said "yes" and was so glad I did. In our last few years, he would come up behind me when I was sitting in my chair, kiss me on the top of the head, and say, "Verne, you'll never know how much I love you." How I miss those moments.

CHAPTER TWO:
SMALL TOWN BOYS

I was born during World War II in a small town in western Pennsylvania named Lynnwood. At the time, my home was on a section of a farm owned by the Lynn family. The name "Lynn" had strong ties to our country's first president, George Washington. After the Revolutionary War, General Washington owned thousands of acres in Western Pennsylvania. He had acquired the land while he was surveying at Fort Necessity in the Appalachian Mountains, near the Maryland border. He looked over the land and layed out plans for a town, which was later called Perryopolis. Washington planned the town as taking the form of a wagon wheel. He hoped that it might be chosen as the site of our nation's capital. After the War, when another site was selected, he divided the land in half and gave the parcels to two of his trusted colonels who had fought with him. One was Colonel Andrew Lynn and the other was Colonel John Cook. My grandmother was one of 13 children of Colonel Lynn's great-great-grandson.

When my grandmother, Nellie, (who I called Mom-Mom) and her siblings were growing up, they would picnic on a section of the farm that they called Lynne's Woods. Later, my grandmother and her sister, Emma, bought 50 acres from their father and built their houses there after they married. Thus, Lynnwood was founded. In 1898, Nellie married a widower, Vernon Leslie Everett, from Ohio. They moved to Oregon, but wound up coming back to Nellie's family farm in Pennsylvania.

Nellie and Vern tried to start a family but she suffered a miscarriage and then was unable, or afraid, to try another pregnancy. They finally decided to try adoption, and adopted a

Verne's grandparents
and Verne

Verne's grandparents

newborn girl from Jamestown, Pennsylvania. They named her Evelyn Margaret Everett. She was beautiful and she and Vern bonded immediately. Unfortunately, Nell and Evelyn had a stormy relationship from the beginning. There had been rumors that Vern had an affair with another woman and had gotten her pregnant. Whether this influenced Nellie's behavior toward their adopted newborn, or the "adopted" baby was actually the child her husband had with his mistress, is unclear. But, from day one, there were issues between the two, and those issues would go on to greatly influence my life as well.

The relationship between them only grew worse as Evelyn got older and in time, she started to hate her mother. This was not without provocation. Nellie was a very stern, righteous and religious woman and she imposed many restrictions on Evelyn. These included rather cruel ones such as making her wear outdated pantaloons and beating her with a stick if she did not do as she was told. The bond between mother and daughter fractured, while the bond between Vern and Evelyn grew stronger. Any hope of reconciliation was shattered when Nellie refused to allow Evelyn to marry her first love, who was from a prominent Belle Vernon family, because he was Catholic. The young lovers were not allowed to see each other again, and Evelyn was tormented both by the loss of her young beau and the fact that she could not escape her mother.

Nineteen-year-old Evelyn eventually was introduced to a nice young Baptist from the nearby town of Donora and he was smitten with her. Evelyn saw her way out and so she and John Harold Stump eloped.

They found a small apartment in Belle Vernon and initially, were happy—John because he had a beautiful young wife, and Evelyn because she was free. In a matter of a few months, she became pregnant and John was ecstatic, but the newlyweds soon began to struggle.

Verne's mother, Evelyn Stump

Because he worked at a steel mill, John was deferred from the draft. The country was not yet at war, but everyone knew it was coming. Evelyn knew nothing about running a household and was in over her head. She had never been taught to cook and Nellie had not communicated anything to her to prepare her for the duties of being a wife and mother. In her seventh month of pregnancy, she was moving furniture around in her bedroom and went into labor. John rushed her to the hospital where she gave birth to me on September 17, 1940.

In 1940, premature babies were given low odds for survival. My mother was so devastated and weakened by my birth that she was unable to even pick me up. My Grandmother and Grandfather, known to me as Mom-Mom and Pop-Pop, and all of John's sisters — of which there were eight — took over.

Dads sister, Lillian, lovingly referred to as "Baby Fats," would chew food and then feed it to me. (In those days, there were no prepared baby foods or formulas, especially not out in rural areas.) After my release from the hospital, my aunt Mary, known as "Statta Babba," had a baby when Evelyn did, so she nursed me as well as her child. Mom-Mom took our family in because Evelyn knew nothing about caring for a very fragile baby. Pop-pop hastily converted their chicken coop into a one-bedroom house (it was a pretty big coop), so we would all be close to Mom-Mom. Once we all moved in, the battle over little baby Verne started in earnest! Nellie finally had a baby she could love as she had never loved before. The older I got, the more she clung — I could do no wrong! Evelyn resented Nellie giving so much love to her baby and her resentment of her mother began to spill over onto me. Because the two homes were only a few hundred yards apart, Evelyn easily knew everything that my grandparents did and their unconditional love for me made her angry.

As she grew more and more unhappy, she took her misery out on my father. John could do nothing to please her and my earliest memories of them are the bitter fights — hours of yelling, screaming, and my mother throwing things at my dad. John started going out a lot to get away from the rages. Finally, Pop-Pop financed a truck for dad so that he could work for a firm that allowed him to be on the road for weeks at a time. This made it worse for me because without my dad there, I took the brunt of my mom's anger. Adding fuel to the fire was the fact that I could do no wrong in the eyes of her mother. It was a cruel twist, given the fact that when she was a little girl, and so in need of love, she could do nothing right.

By the time I started kindergarten, Evelyn demanded that I do the housework and the dishes after school and on weekends. I had to do these chores before I could go outside and play. I used to sneak out of the house before she was out of bed and run as fast as I could to Mom-Moms. When my mother found me gone, she would telephone but Mom-Mom would say she hadn't seen me. This didn't help me when I finally did show up back at my house. Since mom didn't cook, my dad usually did all the cooking when he was home. But when he was on the road, I had all my suppers with Mom-Mom and Pop-Pop. I learned at a very, very young age how to play the game and stir the waters between Mom-Mom and my mother, and between my parents.

During my youth, every Sunday after church, Mom-Mom, Pop-Pop and I would get in the car and drive the half mile to the Lynn farmhouse where Mom-Mom's brothers, my Uncle Joe and Uncle Sumner, lived. (She called them "the boys.")

The brothers never married and lived in the red brick house all their lives. There was a long lane running from the dirt road up past the house. It then curved gently down a small hill, past the springhouse, curved again and went up past two great white barns to the top of the hill.

Mom-Mom would cook our Sunday dinner and we would then all sit on the side porch. The "boys" would sit me on their laps and tell stories of when they were young and how big the farm was then.

I remember sitting on the long porch that ran along one side of the huge brick house, and eagerly listening to those tales. One of my Uncle's favorites was about George Washington. While leading 12,000 troops during the Whiskey Rebellion of 1794, Washington stopped here and sat under the old locust tree, which still stands in the front yard. The President was visiting Colonel Andrew Lynn, who had served under him during the Revolutionary

War. It was exciting to think that a true American hero had once been here and had such real connections to our family.

After these stories of long ago were finished, Pop-Pop and my uncles would take their afternoon naps. Mom-Mom and I would pack a light snack and walk up the lane, heading past the old barns where the two plow horses, Old Ned and Young Abe, lived. They would stick their funny, whiskered noses out the barn door, give a snort and then go back to eating their hay. I felt like they were telling us, "This is Sunday; we don't plow on Sunday."

We would walk to the top of the hill and, from there, we could see the original Lynn farm house. It was very old and made of dark logs that were almost black and bigger around than I was. The windows were gone and we couldn't go in because the floors, or what were left of them, were very rotten. The old dark house smelled like moss and in places, moss did clung to the sides like a bright green dress. Mom-Mom would take her old red pen knife out of her apron pocket and we would start looking for Indian arrow heads. There were not many to be found because she, her sisters and brothers, and all the kids before them, had been doing this all of their lives. They had a shoe box full of them.

Mom-Mom would say we needed to be very quiet and listen to the past. In that quiet space, I felt I could hear the Indians screaming, feel the arrows whooshing past, and hear the women whispering to the children to lie on the floor away from the windows. If it were a TV show, then suddenly, Roy Rogers, on his horse, Trigger, would have come roaring over the hill, guns blazing. The Indians would turn and flee and everyone would be saved. But real history wasn't like that and in that old cabin, you felt some residual fear from those old, desperate days.

After digging for arrow heads, we would walk up the hill behind the log cabin, sit down and have our snack. We liked to watch the steamboats going up the Monongahela River, far below us. It was a peaceful way to spend a Sunday afternoon.

On our way back to the main house, we always stopped at the springhouse where we would collect butter and cream for my uncles, then it would be time to leave.

These memories are the most pleasant of my childhood. In my early life, Mom-Mom was the one that showed me love no matter what I did to displease her. I loved Pop-Pop in a different way. Evelyn was extremely close to her father and discouraged any loving relationship we might have had. If I did anything to make her mad, like if I broke a dish while doing the dishes (which happened frequently for I had to stand on a stool to reach the sink), she would scream and holler. She would then get on the phone and call Pop-Pop and tell him to come down and bring a switch. He would come, take me out on the lawn, and with a twinkle in his eyes, give a couple of light taps and say, "Leave her alone for a while and she will calm down." Evelyn never ventured into Mom-Mom's house unless she had to.

Today, the log cabin and barns are long gone; Mom-Mom, Pop-Pop and my uncles passed decades ago, but the brick house is still there and it is still beautiful.

Most important, are what remains — wonderful memories of these people and that time in my childhood. I have few good memories of my growing up, but these I treasure. I also have two Indian arrow heads!

When I was seven, Mom got pregnant and John decided to add another bedroom. I had been sleeping on the couch or in the big house with Pop-Pop. By the time my brother, John Everett Stump or "Jack" was born, my new bedroom was finished. For a year we shared it, but Evelyn decided it was too small for two. She also thought I might be a bad influence on her little Jack, so I was sent to the big house to sleep with Pop-Pop again. At the big house, they still had Evelyn's former bedroom which was never used, so Mom-Mom gave it to me. Evelyn was furious and refused to speak to her mother for months. It was only after Pop-Pop convinced

Evelyn that she was hurting Nellie that she started to speak to her mother again — and even that gesture was more for my grandfather's sake than Mom-Mom's. She never forgave me for sleeping in her room.

Verne's father, John Harold
Stump, and Verne as a baby

*Verne's dad and
a cousin*

Verne's sister Tippy and brother Jack

By this time, I was in grade school which was located in the town of Fairhope where the Lynn farmhouse stood. Occasionally, I would walk to the farm and say "hi "to Uncle Joe and Uncle Sumner. When I stopped by, sometimes Uncle Joe would give me a quarter. I would then go to old man Callelly's general store and buy Mom-Mom a tiny little kerosene lamp.

Mom-Mom would be so pleased when I gave it to her that her whole face would just light up. This went on for a while and Mom-Mom displayed all the lanterns proudly on the kitchen sideboard. One day, she ask Evelyn to come up to get a casserole she had fixed because she knew John was going to be home and it was his favorite. While Evelyn was in the kitchen, Mom-Mom proudly pointed out the kerosene lamps I had given her. Evelyn demanded to know where I got the money but I wouldn't tell her. I didn't want her to know I was stopping to see Uncle Joe.

The next day, after school she took me into old man Callelly's store and said she was returning the lamps I stole. He said, "Mrs. Stump, Vernon Lynn didn't steal them, he paid for them." I never did tell her where I got the money although she always swore I had stolen it. Mom-Mom was happy to get the lanterns back and never forgave her daughter for her actions. This was just one of the many times that Evelyn showed that she distrusted me.

The worst thing about my relationship with my mother was the ridicule. As far back as I can remember, and I'm going back to about the age of 2 ½, she made fun of me. I was still in a crib at that age, for I was still very small, and the crib was in a corner of the bedroom and adjacent to the living room. There was a door next to my crib and I could see from one room to the other. I was playing with my penis as little boys sometimes do, and both my parents were watching and laughing. They both fondled me and when I would get an erection they would laugh again. I felt like I was doing something to please them. Sex seemed very important to them, so from an early age, it seemed important to me, too, even though I was too young to really know what those feelings were. I spent most of my early life staying with Mom-Mom and Pop-Pop and I had to sleep with my Pop-Pop. He would wrestle with me at bedtime and I enjoyed looking up his nightgown and seeing his penis. These behaviors by some of the adults in my life added to the mixed emotions I was having about sex.

The feelings I had for my mother were even more confused. For all she persecuted me, she could also show such love and be so funny. When I was very small, I remember her running the vacuum (which she hated) and singing a song which was on the radio. Suddenly, she swooped me up in her arms and smothered me with kisses. But then, while I was still overjoyed about this affection, she just as quickly turned and sent me to bed, as if I'd done something to make her mad. I have blocked out much of my childhood memories because when I try to remember, it is very, very painful.

Life pretty much stayed the same until I entered junior high, and then my life changed very fast. By now our family had expanded to include my brother, Jack and my sister, Tippy, who was born when I was 10. I realized in junior high, and even before that, that I liked boys and I liked to "mess around' as we called it. I dated girls sometimes and even had sex with a few but I liked boys much better. In high school, my cousin introduced me to Louise and told me she was a good f---k, which really didn't matter to me by then. What did intrigue me was the fact that my mother couldn't stand her. I was now living full time with Mom-Mom and Pop-Pop and sleeping in Evelyn's old room. Evelyn disliked Louise so much, and I now disliked my mother so much, that I proposed to Louise while in my senior year. I knew the moment Louise said "yes" that I had made a huge mistake but I did not know how to get out of it. Looking back, I realize now, that although the marriage was a mistake, I don't regret that it happened. Louise and I had a beautiful little boy together named Robert; when he was 18, he came back

Verne's son Robert
at 18

Robert and his wife Sue
and baby Jennifer.
(Robert and Sue now have
two children.)

Verne's granddaughter, Jen and her husband David

Verne's grandson James

Verne's three great-grandchildren, Hannah, Emma, & Ally

into my life and I now have a relationship with a wonderful son, my two grandchildren and three great-grandchildren.

That wasn't the only drastic decision I made my senior year— I enlisted in the Air Force, mostly to piss off my mother. This decision upset everyone because Mom-Mom and Pop-Pop planned to pay for college, but it was too late, I was committed.

I left for basic training in Texas right after graduation. On my first leave, I went home and married Louise. I was then sent to pharmacy tech school in Alabama. During tech school, I found an apartment and went home to fetch my wife. All seemed to go well for the first year of our marriage — I even stayed away from boys. I fell in love with a couple but I didn't touch them. Then our son, Robert Lynn, was born, and things started to go bad. We had moved back to Texas and had a little trailer home. Being in the service, I was surrounded by men and some started to hang out at our trailer.

I didn't mess around with my Air Force friends, but I would sneak out after my wife went to bed and find boys to satisfy my needs. Our best friend was a fellow medic named Guy and when Robert was about 1½ we vacationed with Guy, Russell, another young man I was madly in love with, and my wife. Louise never suspected that I was involved with Russell or any other young men, even though I was rarely sleeping with her. If I had a boyfriend, I didn't sleep with her. If I didn't have one, I would sleep with her just because I enjoyed sex. It sounds cruel, but that was my mindset in those days.

We had planned on staying with Guy's mother in Denver for a few days then would head to Lake Louise in Canada. Because I had Russell with me, Guy's mother would not let him stay in her house. This was not because he was gay, but simply because she towed a very hard line. (Guy was adopted and also had a difficult life.) She was not expecting another guest and so would not accommodate one. I made the "sacrifice" and agreed to stay in Guy's cousin's apartment, which was empty, with Russell. I never had sex with him, but we slept together a lot which was all I needed at the time.

After the vacation, Louise and I started to fight all the time. I was very unhappy with my life and even slapped her once. She called her brother and he drove down to Texas and took her and

Verne and wife Louise

Robert back to Pennsylvania. I couldn't afford to live by myself; I did not have enough income without the allotment I received for my wife and child. Rescue came in the form of Russell's mother, who thought she was in love with me. Bizarre as it sounds, she invited me to move in and said I could share her son's bed. I felt I had it all — Louise and Robert were home where her parents wanted them anyway, and away from me, and I was sleeping with my Russell. This went on for six months but then the Air Force found out that I was not living in the apartment with my family as approved. I was ordered to move back on base.

I had already been busted a year before for using drugs from the pharmacy where I worked. I had started taking Dextroamphet-amine capsules which gave me incredible energy and allowed me to work my ass off all day long; the problem was that then I need to take Quaaludes at night to calm down. I'd been doing this for three years and was now addicted. If I didn't work at the pharmacy, my supply would be cut off, and I was feeling desperate. I attempted suicide by taking every pill I could get my hands on. Russell found me and I was saved. I didn't want to die, but I was clearly making a cry for help. When Louise heard, she came back, with Robert, to try and be there for me, but things went from bad to worse.

Poor Louise had no idea what was going on with me. She tried everything she could to cope with my mood swings. Thankfully, Guy was still our friend and he did all he could to shelter my wife and my son. Unknown to all, I started being a peeping tom to get my jollies. I had long been a voyeur and the need for the sexual gratification that I got from peeping was too strong for me to ignore.

At one of the homes I had spied on several times, I found a tire gauge on the sidewalk in front of the house. I picked it up and put it in my pocket. This was Friday June 13, 1963 and I had one week to go before my Air Force discharge on June 20th. I had been told by a good friend, who worked in Personnel, that my discharge would be a general under honorable conditions because I had been busted and had the suicide attempt; this didn't bother me — I just wanted out! People in the house where I was caught claimed that someone had come into their house in the past and took some tools and $20.00 in cash. I told them it wasn't me but when they searched my house the next day, they found the tire gauge. They claimed the gauge had been with the tools that were stolen. The arresting officer said, "Son, because you have no record, if you plead 'guilty,' you'll get probation and will be fine." I was so scared that I did what he said.

Unfortunately, he was wrong. I was put in jail, and because of the offense, I was put in a cell with hardened criminals. There were two cells in my block, each with 10 men, and when I entered the men in the next cell started hollering "fresh meat, fresh meat." I knew that if those men got hold of me I would be gang raped. On my second night after showers, I went back to my cell. Those men worked it out with the guard to have me put in their cell and even had my mattress already moved to their cell. When I realized what was happening, I escaped the cell just as the guard was closing the gate so I was left in the corridor. The guard laughed but he did open my old cell and another guy shared his cot with me.

The next morning, at breakfast, four of the prisoners beat the hell out of me and the man who had shared his cot. The guards just laughed. That morning, I wrote to Louise and told her I was going to commit suicide, knowing it would be censored. That afternoon, I was taken to the warden's office where he apologized. He said I should never been placed with the hardened prisoners and moved me to the first floor where an older man of 40 took me under his protection. I spent three months in jail before I was given 10 years of probation. I was allowed to take my wife and son back to Pennsylvania, and report to an officer there.

I was, and still am, grateful that Louise stuck by me, but I'm not sure she understood why all these problems kept happening.

When we arrived home, we had no place to live, so my father took us in. This was just the excuse that Evelyn needed to move in with Pop-Pop. Sadly, Mom-Mom had died on June 22nd, while I was in jail. I hope that she never knew what had happened to her "little boy."

Dad found us an apartment in public housing, got me into a tech training program, and then gave me a job. My future looked grim at this point. Dad also talked to my probation officer. He knew everybody in the area because he had been a constable for many years. The probation officer said, "Don't worry, Vernon Lynn, will be fine," but that was not the case.

Louise and I were not happy. My son was turning four and he was adorable. I worried — can I trust myself when he gets older?

Then I met Gary and fell madly in love. This time, I acted on my feelings and we had great sex. I no longer tried to avoid having a relationship. Soon after, I was doing some painting at our house. I was moving furniture and happened on three letters in Louise's drawer — they were from Guy. He had cared for her and Robert while I was in jail and in the letters, he told her how much he loved her and Robert. He wished that someday they could all be together. Guy's letters showed me my way out but I could also see my family's happiness before me. That weekend, I took her and Robert to her mother's to do the wash and never went back for them. I did not say good-bye. When she called to say she was ready for me to pick her up, I said, "I'm not coming back. Stay there. Live your life."

Within six weeks she had a divorce and was married to Guy. Robert has two step-sisters, whom he loves dearly, and he got to grow up in a loving, stable home. I did not see him during his youth, although I thought of him often. I know there were several points where he wanted to contact me, but I wasn't ready and did not return his overtures. I was not sure if he really wanted to see me or if he would keep trying to find me, but I felt that one day, he would.

When the time came, I would be ready. As it turned out, he came back into my and Clay's lives in 1980 and we have been in touch ever since. On his first visit, when we were in Boston, he and my sister, Tippy spent two wonderful weeks with Clay and me. Before he left, I asked him what his mother had told him about my being gay and my past and he said she had never told him anything. I've never asked her why. I also learned that while Louise didn't want Robert to visit me, Guy told him to "follow his heart," and they did not stand in the way of his finding me.

*Robert and his
new father, Guy*

*Robert and
his mother, Louise*

I should note here that when I met Clay, I told him that I had a record. He knew that if I made one little step out of line, I would go to prison — and for quite awhile. He also knew that I was addicted to peeping, that I had not stopped peeping even after we were together, and that even the threat of prison hanging over me was not enough of a deterrent. He tried everything to get me to stop, but nothing worked. For so many years, despite his love, I just seemed to be on this path to self-destruction. I continued to roll the dice not just with my future, but our future, every time I took these risks — yet he never walked away. After a time, I did stop peeping, but it took quite awhile. I'll never fully understand why Clay stayed with me but he did.

In 1964, Gary and I decided to move in together. We also wanted to join a friend of mine from high school who lived in Florida. I went to my probation officer for permission and he said, "Do what you want, you're clean." All I could think of was, "Thank you, dad, for helping me get this behind me!"

Life in Florida was quite an experience. Gary was 16 and I was 24 and neither of us had any work experience that could land us decent jobs. I had car payments and we needed rent money. We also needed to find a place to rent. I had assumed that my high school friend would greet me with open arms, find me a job, and a place to live. WRONG!! He did not want any people from his past life intruding on his current situation. He had made his own way and was becoming very successful. Somehow, we found an apartment to share with a nice gay man. This lasted for about two months.

Then, we found a sugar daddy who worked for an airline, was married, and wanted a little cuddling now and then from both of us. By then, I had found a job as a shoe salesgirl and was making decent money. With 'daddy's" help, we could afford a place of our own. This pattern of finding a place to live, then moving, lasted for a year or so and created some stress in our relationship. We also both indulged in affairs, which led to real fights — the kind that resulted in broken arms and leg, black eyes, and so on.

By this time, I had a better job as a project scheduler for a paper company and Gary had his own sugar daddy (our pilot had flown) who was willing to kick in when needed. We were able to purchase a very nice mobile home and found a great lot near the ocean. Life was going okay for Gary and me. My whole family came for a visit — my mother, new father (Evelyn and John had finally divorced and she had remarried), my sister and her boyfriend, and my brother and his wife. We swam in the ocean at night and had a great four days. Life was good.

A short time later, we met another gay couple and became very close to them. One was the CEO of a small corporation and the other was a nurse, who kept us clap free. By 1966/67, life began to get very muddled. I met a man named Bob, who was in the Air Force and wanted to move off base. He would stay overnight and sleep with Gary and me. This went on for a very short period and then we agreed he could live in our spare room. He moved some of his things in and then decided that he was in love with me, which for me, was not part of the plan. Bob also made remarks that disturbed me. A few times when we went driving together we crossed a small bridge with a concrete abutment; on these occasions he would say, "Sometimes when I'm depressed I just want to run my car into that bridge." The second weekend after he moved in, he wanted to go to a gay bar in town but neither Gary nor I wanted to go, so he went by himself. About midnight he called, and I could tell he had too much to drink. He was crying and telling me how much he loved me and begged me to come to the bar. I said "No," and he screamed that if I didn't, he would kill himself. I did not go and he never came home. The next morning, we heard on the news that he had driven into the bridge abutment and was in intensive care at the hospital. He died two days later. To this day, I sometimes ask myself if I could have prevented it.

After Bob's death, everything seemed to fall apart. Bob's father came down but he was in a wheelchair and quite helpless so Gary and I offered to go to Pennsylvania with him and Bob's body. They lived 50 miles from where my mother lived, so my mother and her husband came to see us. After the funeral, we spent a few days with them in Belle Vernon. This was not a good time for any of us. My mother started accusing us of stealing her pots and pans when we moved to Florida and this turned into a massive fight that lasted two days. When we returned to Florida, our best friends told us that they were moving to Ohio and wanted us to join them. The CEO said he would have our trailer moved to Ohio at no cost to us. I quit my job; Gary never did have a decent job so had nothing to lose, and off to Columbus, Ohio we went.

By now it was early 1968. Within a few months of our move, Gary and I were at the end of our relationship. I found a job immediately but was let go after the probation period because I wore flashy shirts and ties. One good thing that came of the job was that while there, I met Doug and fell madly in love. Gary went back to his mother. Doug and I had three sex-filled love months but then I caught him cheating on me. I had warned Doug that if I ever caught him cheating it was over and I was going back to Gary.

I sent Doug packing, called Gary, and he returned. You might wonder why Gary came back, but in fact, I was the only person who treated him with any respect or caring — that and I had a convertible. I also think he was not happy at his mom's! Meanwhile, I had found a very good job as comptroller for a trucking company in Columbus and was starting to have a good time again. A girl who worked for me said she was in love with me so she and her best friend, who was from a very wealthy family, started hanging out with me and Gary. They knew we were gay but didn't seem to care; maybe they thought they could convert us! By now, Gary was starting to realize that his best asset was in his pants. He got the best friend pregnant and they got married. I was pissed at Gary's actions, but could see that this was his ticket to a comfortable life. He was happy with the relationship because at heart, he was a gold digger and now he could enjoy an easy, wealthy lifestyle. The other girl still wanted to marry me, but I'd been there and done that, and wasn't going there again.

Not long after, around Christmas of 1968, I made my second suicide attempt by slitting my wrists. I still have the scars. I don't remember who found me. I was upset over Gary and was just feeling very lost and alone. After that, the next few months were wild. I remember that I fell in love with three different men during that period. I don't know if I was just young, desperate or searching or maybe all three. The sex kept me going, kept me alive. That spring, enter Clay! And everything changed.

When I look back over my life, I often think it's a miracle that I turned out as well as I did — I could easily have led a sordid life, given how I was treated as a child and all that happened. I also know it's a miracle that I survived. If I had not met Clay when I did, I know I would have died young. He was my salvation and he knew it — I think that's why he never left me.

Clay's Growing Up

I had the honor of being Clay's partner and lover for 45 years, so I feel that I'm qualified to tell the story of his life before I came along. Clay was born in a small town called Perry in upstate New York. Clay's birth date is February 27, 1936. He was the second oldest of five. He often joked that his mother had two boys, two girls and him. His mother's father was Joe Hanley and when Clay was in his teens, his grandfather was lieutenant governor of

Clay's grandmother, Gammy

Clay as a child

New York under Governor Tom Dewey. Dewey ran for president in 1948 against Harry Truman, and Joe knew that if Dewey won, he would win the subsequent election for governor. Clay's mother, Jody, was Joe's chief of staff and was also managing his campaign; his uncle Julian was a New York Supreme Court judge, so his family was very prominent in the state. Unfortunately for Joe, Dewey lost, and that loss would take a toll on Clay's family later.

Clay's father, Ken Wilcox, ran a small dairy farm and was consumed with trying to make a living and support his growing family. Growing up, Clay saw both sides of the coin — the power of working in government and the hard physical work of running a farm.

Clay at his family's dairy farm with
his mother, Jody, and his older brother, Jim

Clay had an older brother Jim, and a sister, Nora, who was 18 months younger. She was the love of his life. They just had a special connection. In later years, after she was married and divorced, we helped support Nora; we also had her come for an extended visit every year so that she could have a vacation. Sadly, she had diabetes and died at age 64. Clay also had a younger brother, Jeff, and a little sister, Kate, who was much younger, and whose arrival was a surprise to all.

When Clay was very young, his mother realized that he was very intelligent. She also considered him her favorite, or as Clay joked, "the pick of the litter." Because of this, he was encouraged to study so he could get into college. This meant that his older brother had to do more work on the farm and because of this, he resented Clay all of his life.

Clay as a young boy

*Clay's father, Ken and
Clay's niece, Katie
at four years old*

Clay at 12

Clay knew early on that he was gay. In his early teens, he was "brought out" by a young man who worked on the farm and so he never had sex with women. In his late teens, he used to go down to Boston and spend the weekend in the gay bars. He'd get home to the farm around 3 a.m. only to find his dad in the kitchen already having breakfast. His father would say, "I hope it was worth it. Eat breakfast and I'll see you in the barn for 4 a.m. milking."

By the time Clay entered college at Syracuse University, his grandfather had retired from state office. He had racked up quite a bit of debt during his failed campaign for governor, but Uncle Julian made sure the debts were paid. Joe Hanley was never the same after that; he was depressed and also went blind and almost deaf — a sad state for a once powerful man. Clay's mother felt disgraced and never got over it. The final blow came when the farm had to be sold. The farm was successful with 50 or 60 cows, but Clay's grandfather was always seeking status and built it up to 100 cows. This was too much work, too much feed, too much of everything to sustain. Ken tried but ultimately found himself going broke, so the farm had to be sold.

After the farm was sold, the Catholic Church gave Ken and Jody jobs as caretakers of a cemetery and a place to live. The

Clay in high school

Church recognized Clay's family as long-standing pillars of the community and wanted to help in some fashion.

After Clay graduated with a degree in audiology, he got a job in Irvine, California at a school teaching deaf children. All seemed to be going well until he was arrested for having sex in a roadside rest area. The incident caused him to lose his job. Depressed, he came back East and found another teaching job in Buffalo, New York but when his record caught up with him, he lost that one as well. Much defeated and very ashamed of letting his family down, Clay went back to living with them and working at the cemetery. He spent the next two years digging graves beside his father. He always said that these were two of the best years of his life because he got to know his father and realized what a great man he was.

He also discovered how much his father loved him. During his early years, his father was so busy trying to put food on the table and take care of his family, that he had spent little time with his kids. Now, he and Clay had a chance to really talk and be together.

Those two years helped Clay regain his self-confidence and he eventually moved to Cleveland, Ohio. Once there, he started graduate school at Case Western Reserve University. Before he could present his thesis for his Ph.D, he was hired by Ohio State University in Columbus, Ohio to teach graduate students in the Audiology Department. He had met a few gay friends while in graduate school, but he was very afraid of getting into trouble again. He had met his boyfriend, Mike there, so when he moved to Columbus to teach, he would go back to Cleveland on the weekends to stay with him. However, Clay claimed it was never a serious relationship.

That was fortunate for me because soon thereafter, we met!

Clay with his sister, Kate, and her husband, Harold

Clay's younger brother, Jeff, with Clay's nephew, Josh (now Abigail)

Clay and his niece, Katie

Clay's sister Nora

Clay and Verne in the '70s

*Clay playing piano
in Columbus*

CHAPTER THREE:
THE COLUMBUS YEARS: 1968-1973

Clay and I met in 1968 in Columbus, Ohio, in a gay bar named The Cat's Meow. When he first saw me, I was dancing on the bar with nothing on but a red purse and a pair of red, four-inch, Joan Crawford fuck-me heels. I was living at the time with a crazy, fun-loving kid named Glen. Clay was a professor at Ohio State University in the Audiology Department, teaching grad students. It was the year before Woodstock and being gay was not easy. Police would regularly raid the two main gay bars in town and if you were caught touching, or, God forbid, dancing, you were immediately arrested. They took down license plate numbers in the parking lot and published names in the papers. Many friends lost good jobs because of this.

I've always been keen on cars, and Clay had a new TR6. (I had an old Ford Fairlane.) When I met Clay, all I could think was, "Wow, Verne! He has a neat car and is a college prof! Jackpot!" I had my little group of friends at the time and I was "queen bee." Clay was soon part of our group and everybody thought he was so cute. After awhile, he worked up the courage to ask me if I knew where he could get some dope, meaning weed. "Of course," I said, and we were off and running. Things went slow at first: dinner, drinks, theater, etc. I didn't want to scare him off.

Glen, my bedmate at the time, thought Clay was cute, too. Before Clay came on the scene, my friendship with Glen had been slowly growing. In May of 1970, we had moved into a small one-bedroom apartment in the German Village section of Columbus. One Friday night, Glen took my car and went to the Cat's. I was painting and didn't want to go. Glen brought the car home at about 1:00 a.m. and told me that he was going to a party that a queen I couldn't stand was giving. He knew I wouldn't want to go and he was gone all night. The next night, Saturday, I went to the Cat's without Glen, who preferred to stay home. Clay was there.

After a few dances and a lot of drinks, Clay finally asked (it had been over a year of dating, mind you) if I would go home with him and spend the night. As we were discreetly leaving the bar, the gang, in unison, hollered "good night, girls!" The next morning, as Clay was fixing breakfast (added bonus: he loved to cook), his phone rang. After talking for a few minutes, Clay said, "He's here. Do you want to talk to him?" It was Glen. I learned that he had slept with Clay the night before!

Let me take a moment to say, that while it may seem that we were very casual with our relationships, it was more a sign of the times. In those days, before Aids, if you were young and gay, you lived life full on and partied hard. You just wanted to have fun, and if you found love along the way, all the better. I was mostly in party mode — I wasn't expecting love.

The next weekend, Clay was going to a contra dance workshop near where my mother, Evelyn, lived. He took me to visit her while he went dancing. From then on, she and I had another reason to resent each other. Clay was everything she had hoped to find: he was good looking, a college professor and had money (although it turned out that part was wrong).

After he dropped me off at my mom's, he got a notification from his Ph.D. advisor at Case Western Reserve telling him that his Ph.D. advisory committee was available for his dissertation review. (He already had a position at OSU, but had not presented his final dissertation at Case Western.) He wouldn't have this opportunity again for another year. He asked my mother if she would take me home the next day so that he could go do his dissertation. I received a collect phone call on Monday asking if I would accept a call from a Dr. J. Clayton Wilcox. I did and from that day on, we never spent a night apart. Let the stories begin!

By the end of June, we had decided that we didn't need two apartments. Clay's was very expensive and out in the 'burbs, so we stored his furniture and he moved in with me. Glen understood that our relationship was over and wasn't sure whether to be mad at me or at Clay. For spite, he enlisted in the Air Force. He was always a bit impulsive.

We started to search for a two-bedroom apartment in German Village, which was the most expensive part of town. Clay had two cats, Wafe and Chomus, and I had a dog named Fe-Fe that I had inherited, along with the clap, from my last lover. Clay fell in love with Fe-Fe but I had to get over the clap. Win some, lose some, as they say!

We were getting pretty discouraged with our apartment hunt in the Village when I ran into a friend who lived next door. Mickie owned a brick two-story house located on the back end of his lot. He told us that the house was empty. He hadn't received any rent from the four girls who supposedly lived there for over two years, and he had not even been in it for over a year. He said that if we wanted to look at it, he'd take us through.

What we found was a real shock. The girls living on the first floor were long gone, as were the girls on the second. The water heater on the second floor had failed. The resulting steam had caused all the wallpaper in the entire house to come off. The place was a disaster. Mick said that he could not possibly rent it to anyone. We made him an offer to rent it "as is." We would do the work to make it livable or pay to have it restored. He was so surprised (as was Clay), that we were willing to do such a thing that he offered to rent it to us for $75.00 a month, and he agreed to pay for everything we did. We moved in on July 1st. On the 4th of July, we had our first party.

It was a wonderful old brick house. We gave all of my friends a sledge hammer, took all the plaster off the brick on one wall in the living room, the dining room and kitchen, and then had the brick sandblasted and pointed. That was the start of many projects in our first house. By the time we moved three years later, we had redone the kitchen with custom-made, in-place cabinets, put in a commercial-grade indoor barbecue pit, and had a six-foot copper hood installed above the stove.

I think I heard Clay give a sigh of relief, hoping that I wasn't going to tell some of the Columbus stories, but bitch that

I am, here goes! Some, when I retold them, he laughed at; some made him smile, and some made him leave the room.

We started entertaining before all of the renovations were even done. For our first Thanksgiving dinner together, we had invited four friends to dine with us. On Monday I picked out an expensive paper for the dining room walls — and ceiling. Yes, ceiling. I got the walls done Monday and Tuesday, and started the ceiling early Wednesday morning. By noon, we had one strip up. Then it fell off. Clay's ex-lover hung wall paper, so he called him and he came over to help. We worked all night. Clay only stopped to put the turkey in the oven and of course, by then, we had added two more people for dinner — Clay's ex and his new beau. The room got done, as did the turkey, most of us had fun, but Clay went to bed right after desert. He was exhausted! This story he laughed at.

The next major event is hard to tell, even after 46 years, but my intention with this story is to be as honest as I can be. It showed me what it was like to be loved for the first time in my life, and Clay kept showing me for the rest of his life.

It started at 3:00 in the afternoon, February 16th, 1971. Clay was teaching a class at a northern campus and would be getting home about 6:00 p.m. I agreed to have dinner started when he got home and needed to go to the market. On the way home, at a usual cruising spot, a boy I'd had sex with before Clay and I moved in together (and a couple of times after), waved to me. I stopped and he asked if he could come over. I said 'yes' and he did.

When we got to the house, I told him that Clay would be home soon and I had to start dinner. I told him he was welcome to stay and meet Clay and have dinner with us. I fixed us drinks and told him that I needed to go upstairs and headed up with my drink in hand.

I got to the second floor landing and suddenly felt a sharp pain between my shoulder blades. I thought he had hit me. I sat my drink on the steps and turned around. He ran down the stairs and out the door. When I turned around, my back scraped the wall and I realized there was a knife in it.

All I could think of was getting it out and starting dinner before Clay got home. I knew if the police got involved and the story got out, Clay would probably lose his job. I called our neighbors, who were also gay, and ask if they could come over. I said that I needed their help to take a knife out of my back.

They were over the fence and in my kitchen before I could hang the phone up. When they came through the door, I was standing facing them with a dish towel in my hand. Clark said, "Jesus Christ, Verne, cut the joke." They had just been sitting down to dinner. They thought I was making it up and had a fake knife in my back — until they saw the blood puddling on the floor. By this time, we realized we needed to call an EMT. I knew I had to fabricate a story for the cops.

While waiting for the EMT, I hid the kid's coat in a closet, threw out his cigarettes and lighter, washed and put away his glass — and came up with a plausible story. As it turned out, it wasn't that hard. A few weeks before, a man who ran a business across the street was shot and killed in front of our gate. I had come out when I heard them arguing. As I approached the gate, a shot was fired. The shooter looked up at me and said, "If you call anyone, I'll come back and kill you."

I had run back into the house and locked all the doors and windows. I could hear the dying man calling my name, but I was too afraid to even call the police.

I knew the cops were still aware of this and of my involvement, so I told them I had heard a noise outside my door. I went outside and down two steps to take a look but saw nothing. I turned, went back up the steps and was stabbed before I got in the door, which would account for the location and angle of the stab wound in my back.

The EMTs had me walk to the ambulance because they did not dare put me on a stretcher. I had to lay face down on the floor, hoping that nothing would make the knife jiggle. In the emergency room, they started by cutting off my clothes. I begged them not to cut off my belt. It was new and I had gone to the Twin Cities to find it, so they inched me up and slid it off. I kept it for years. Clay finally threw it out. It was marked on the back "2/16/71, keep as evidence, killing, V. Stump"— that was the date of my stabbing.

As they were wheeling me to the elevator for surgery, Clay came in and kissed me and through tears said, "Verne, I love you very much. You have to tell them what really happened. They don't believe you."

"I can't, love," I said. "I love you too much. Whatever happens happens."

I can remember being on the operating table. Suddenly everything turned a beautiful shade of blue and I could hear someone saying, "He's not going to make it. He's stopped breathing" and someone else saying, "Breathe, dammit. Breath dammit." I heard myself saying, "Fuck you!" and then I came around.

The next thing I knew, I was in the recovery room and Clay was holding my hand. He said I had stepped out of this life for a minute. He stayed as long as they would let him. Later, Clay told me that earlier, the surgeon had told him that they did not think that I would make it through the surgery. The knife had severed a major artery and was embedded a fraction of an inch from my heart and up against my spinal column. They had to cut me from the center of my chest up to under my right arm and then up my back to the base of my neck. I once knew how many stitches it was, but I have forgotten. It was a lot.

On the third day, the doctor told Clay that if they could not get me to walk by morning then he should notify family because I probably would not make it. Clay left to go home and start calling. After he left, an elderly black nurse's aid, who was very gentle, said to me, "Honey, your hair's a mess. I'm gonna comb it."

Now I've got to tell it as it was. One of my previous lovers was a hairdresser and decided to make me a really nice hairpiece that I could glue into what hair I did have. The hairpiece was so well done that you would never have guessed I was wearing one. As she combed my hair, it came out because it had not been glued in for days.

Well, that nurse's aid nearly fell off her chair! I think she thought she had scalped me! Once she knew what had happened, she made me get out of bed, walk across the room, pick up the phone and call Clay so he could bring in my glue. All he could do when he answered the phone was cry and say, "Verne, I love you so much."

Clay brought me home from the hospital on his 35th birthday, February 27, 1971 — a day I'll never forget for many reasons. Before he left for class he said, "Remember, love, you have to stay in bed the rest of the day, and all day tomorrow. Now promise."

"Yes, dear," I said. After he left, I got dressed, got in my car, drove downtown, parked, went into Dayton's and bought him a birthday present. It may have been foolish, but his birthday was important to me. The stabbing is one story that neither of us laughs about. We still shed a lot of tears when we remember that time. It caused us to learn a lot about each other very early in our relationship.

A few weeks later, I was following Clay home. He was driving the snazzy red Barracuda convertible and I was in my Ford Fairlane. He turned off Front Street to get over to Bank Street and I was a few cars behind. He did not have to ask why it took me 45 minutes to go half a block when he saw the front end of my car a short while later. As I drove down Front Street, I saw a cute guy walking down the street. The car in front of me stopped but I didn't. The cute guy didn't either. Which brings me to one of the stories where I laugh and he leaves the room.

With the front end of the Fairlane completely wrecked (it ran okay, if a little shaky at times), I decided it needed to be replaced. However, we did not want to spend a lot of money. Of course, Clay still had his nice red convertible so that was an easy decision for him to make! Right, guy.

The next Saturday, Clay had a dance workshop, so I went car shopping. As I passed the Dodge dealership, I noticed a 1966 red Dodge convertible. Then I drove north to the 'burbs where Clay used to live. There, the Olds dealership had a 1968 yellow convertible. I stopped and asked the price — $900. I returned to the Dodge dealer and asked the price for the red one — $600. Okay!

The next Sunday, Clay suggested that we go car shopping, not knowing I already had. We went to the Olds dealer first and saw the yellow convertible. I said, "Clay, I have to have it." On the way home, we just happened to pass the red Dodge convertible, the one I really wanted. Clay said, "There's a nice car. Let's stop." "No," I said, "I want the Olds." We stopped and he "convinced me" that I'd like the Dodge almost as well.

It was quite awhile before Clay heard me tell the full story to someone. After calling me an asshole, he left the room. That was the first time he had ever referred to me in those terms, but it would not be the last. In time, he managed to grin about my car shopping escapade, but he never laughed — and I always got called "you asshole" all over again!

Another unforgettable experience was our first visit to Sheila's together. When we met, Clay felt it was fine to visit friends, as long as you were invited or it had been prearranged. I, on the other hand, was a drop-in kind of guy. Sheila was the account officer for the owner of the company where I worked. Now, bear in mind that this was in the late 1960s and early 1970s. She was a white woman married to a black jazz player and they had two beautiful children. Sheila had hired a beautiful, red-headed Jewish woman who was also married to a black member of the band, to be her assistant. As it turned out, the redhead also had a black boyfriend. Sheila would let them meet in her bedroom. Right after we bought the red Barracuda, I convinced Clay that it would be all right to drop in for a visit with Sheila, to show her the new car. Not long after we got there, we heard a lot of cussing and swearing outside the front door. It was the redhead's husband shouting, "You bitch!" Then he blew the front door in with a shotgun. Clay grabbed my hand, yanked me off the couch, ran for the back door and yelled, "We're outta here."

We didn't do another drop-in for quite a while. Clay learned to laugh at that one — but it took some time!

We enjoyed our time together in Columbus. Mick offered to sell the house to us, but Clay had already accepted a position at the University of Wisconsin in Eau Claire.

Mick sold the place before we left Columbus, and when we left, he presented us with a check for $4,000. We had never paid a penny in rent. The only things he would not reimburse us for were the barbecue pit, the hood and the $20 dollar-per-square-yard plush navy blue carpet. They were not his taste. We took them with us and had them installed in our new home in Eau Claire.

When Clay and I met, I was a comptroller for a large trucking company in Columbus and was making more money than Clay was at OSU. Needless to say, I wasn't exactly a happy camper, having to leave my job and all of our friends in Columbus. Shortly before we moved, my mother called to say she had cancer. Our move to Eau Claire seemed to be getting off to a bad start.

We had our last party and formal dinner on Thanksgiving, 1973, and started packing the next day. We pulled out of Columbus the day after Christmas. We followed the moving van, which was completely full of our stuff, in a red Barracuda which was packed with all of our plants, four adult cats and five five-week-old Siamese kittens. When we arrived in Eau Claire on December 27th, we dropped off the plants and cats at our new digs and then headed to a hotel. The utilities would not be turned until the 28th and it was 32 degrees! We figured the plants and cats would survive. When we awoke at the motel the next morning, it was 28 below! It never got above zero for the next two weeks. We shared a driveway with our neighbors who we waved to when we saw them but because of the weather, we never met them until April.

Thus was our new beginning.

One of our special places was Buckeye Lake. In 1971, before we moved to Eau Claire. We met Jay and Mike at Stillwagons Antique Shop, a favorite stop of ours. They had been together for a few years and were opening their own antique shop, called Little Lake Antiques, about 35 miles south of Columbus on a very, very shallow body of water called Buckeye Lake. It was approximately four feet deep in most areas.

We decided to rent a small cottage on the lake for the summer. It was near the water's edge and snuggled among tall pine trees. If more than four people wanted to join us, they knew they

Clay pulling up zipper at Buckeye Lake

had to bring a tent. Sometimes, there were as many as three white tents between our cottage and the water.

We both were working in town; Clay was teaching summer school and I was at Columbus Retail Delivery. We spent our weekdays going back and forth and our weekends at the lake. We had all the cats there, plus one of the kittens (the others were adopted). By this time, we had quite a few young gay friends. Some I had slept with. Some I had tricked with, but I brought them all into our lives. We loved to entertain, and Clay loved to cook, so we had frequent get-togethers. All of these young men ended up being part of our family. We were their family as well. Two of them are family even now.

Sadly, many of our family died of AIDS later on, but during that summer of '71, they all came to Buckeye. I remember one weekend Clay planned on fixing dinner for five and had brought food from home to cook. Suddenly, people started arriving. There were no cell phones then. In fact, there was no phone at all at Buckeye Lake. After making three trips to a not-so-local and expensive market, he told those who arrived later that they had to go buy what they wanted to eat for the weekend as he was done

Verne and Clay with Barracuda

shopping! He was happy to cook the food for them, but no more running to the market!

One older couple (okay, they were in their forties and fifties) also had a cottage on the lake. They had a large, flat-bottomed boat that could only be used on certain parts of the lake or it would run aground. When they came for dinner, they had to anchor out in the middle of the lake and come ashore in a wooden dingy that they towed behind their boat. It was a sight to behold as they paddled in — they were decked in flowered shirts, wearing large floppy hats decorated with plastic flowers, and waving more flowers. There was a lot of screaming and laughing as they arrived, carrying their casserole dishes to boot. I bet we were talked about by the locals for years. Every time we came to the lake from Columbus we brought something else we thought we had to have. By summer's end, our little cottage had three air conditioners, two TVs, most of Clay's pots and pans, and a large box full of spices.

I was the one who got us our first boat — and what a boat she was — a 1956 Kris Kraft with a Corvette V8 engine, mahogany and leather interior — she was beautiful. She could pull four skiers with ease. How I got her remains something of a mystery; my brother Jack, the used car salesman, was somehow involved, but

I don't recall the details and I never questioned how I wound up with such a boat.

Well, now that we had a boat, we needed dock space on the Olentangy River; we also needed a car heavy enough to pull her, and we had acquired a whole bunch of new friends because we had the boat. We also had to have the boat refinished every year and stored for the winter. Then came the move to Eau Claire, which brought another set of challenges. We had to hire two men with a van to get her to Wisconsin in the middle of winter. Sadly, she never hit the water again but managed to hit the back of our garage a few times before I sold her. I traded her to a man who sold used cars but his real love was classic boats. I made out pretty well, getting a Ford Pinto, a Corvair and a Pontiac wagon in one deal! This allowed Clay and I to each have a winter car — great for this part of the country with its heavy snows — as well as one for fair weather.

Thanks to the wagon, I was also able to help out a friend who was a paraplegic and had a wheelchair. All this time Clay never said that he hated boats; that didn't come up until I bought our second boat, a transaction that brought us close to divorce!

CHAPTER FOUR:
OUR FURRY FAMILY

One of the things that Clay and I had in common was a love for animals. Clay's love was perhaps deeper because he grew up on a farm and had all kinds of them. I only knew cats growing up. They are one of the few things I remember from my childhood that were loving, although one of my early cat memories was very traumatic. One of my first pets was a cat named Rascal; I loved her very much. When she was still young, she had a litter of kittens, which enraged my mom. One day, she called me over and I saw that she had stuffed all of the kittens into a box. She planned to insert the exhaust pipe of our car into the box and kill the kittens and she wanted me to watch. It was like she was punishing me for Rascal having kittens, and, as usual, doing anything she could to hurt me. Mom-Mom found out and ran up crying and begging her to stop. She didn't want me to be there and she didn't want the kittens killed. But my mother wouldn't budge. "Get it done," she said and the kittens were killed. Perhaps that was why I have always felt a special connection to cats. I've had them all my life and they have been among my dearest friends. I have rescued many cats and vowed never again to see a cat or kitten harmed.

When Clay and I met, he had two cats and I had a dog named Fe-Fe. Clay's cats were a Siamese named Clovus and a big, fluffy, black and white cat named Wafe. For the first month we were together, we stayed at Clay's place, because I was still technically living with Glen. By the third week, Glen enlisted in the Air Force and was gone, and sadly, shortly after so was Clovus. He realized that I was never going to leave so he just up and died. Clay and Wafe later moved in with me and Fe-Fe in my tiny apartment.

"Our Cat Family"

Clay with Chuckles

Clay with Cassie in Boston

Comus and Co-Co

One of our Siamese families

This arrangement upset Wafe who started acting funny and not using the litter box. We thought maybe another cat would help so we got Comus, a tiny, male seal point Siamese. Well, Comus tried to make love to Wafe which, of course, made Wafe even more upset. To solve the problem, we got a little female seal point called Cloie.

In the meantime, our cleaning lady, Elsie, took pity on Wafe and brought him home with her. Comus and Cloie then started to make babies — lots of babies, so many that we began to sell them. Thus, while we were still living in Columbus, we formed the "Claver Catery." One tragic upshot of this was that Fe-Fe tried to nurse the kittens, had a heart attack and died! Who would have thought? We kept one of the kittens from the last litter born in Columbus and named her Cassandra, although we called her Cassie for short. In later years, she would curl-up on my drafting table and watch me design.

When we drove to Eau Claire on that cold winter's night, we had Comus, Cloie, Cassie and four kittens in the car. We put an ad in the local paper that we had Siamese kittens for sale for $25.00 apiece. We immediately got a phone call from an irate local woman who raised Siamese and sold her kittens for $75.00 each. How dare we? She told us of a place in Manhattan, New York called "Fabulous Felines" that was devoted to selling pure-bred cats. We contacted them and they told us to ship them the litter and if they met their standards, they would pay us $125.00 apiece. If the cats were not up to par, we would have to pay to have them shipped back. Fortunately, they took that litter and every one thereafter.

In fact, we later put Comus out for stud because he was a very handsome and well-bred boy. One litter yielded a beautiful chocolate point which we kept; we named her Co-Co. She lived to be 24 and died in Portsmouth.

Comus, Cloie, Cassie and Co-Co were our family in the Eau Claire years and into the Boston years. However, Cloie, Cassie and dear old Comus all died before we moved to Portsmouth. Not

Charlie with Cassie

wanting to have Cassie be alone, we added a blue point named Chastity, then after Comus passed, we got another blue point who we called Charlie. Wally, known by all as "The Wahl" came next. Wallie was hurled out of a red SUV at a stoplight when his two female owners were in the midst of a fight. Turns out one liked the cat, the other hated him. I was behind the car and saw the cat get thrown into traffic. As I pulled alongside, without even thinking, I reached out and grabbed the cat by the tail and pulled him in.

I kept the cat hidden in my coat and smuggled him out back and into our jungle-like back porch. I knew I would have to do some fast talking with Clay as to why we needed another cat. He came out to meet the cat — which we first had to find; he was hidden in the plants — but quickly gave in. At first, the big Maine Coon was afraid of all of our Siamese who did not like him one bit. He pretty much stayed in his jungle, so we brought food and water to him. After a few days, he grew bold enough to venture into the kitchen. There was some hissing and puffing up and a lot of sniffing around, but finally the Siamese gave in. "The Wahl" had arrived.

Our other cats were declawed indoor cats, but the Wahl was not declawed and soon figured out how to get out of the house. He became quite the escape artist. We got him a collar that said where he belonged, although he lost it several times. However, frequently people did come by to return either the collar with no cat, the cat with no collar, or sometimes both. We learned that he was well known in other neighborhoods, and in fact, one little girl told us he was called "Stumpy" on her street because the collar said "V. Stump" with our address!

Some years later, Wally went out for one of his sojourns and did not come home. We searched and called but in my heart, I knew he was gone. I still miss him.

A succession of other cats also filled our lives. Dear Henry was a tiny black kitten that I rescued in Dorchester; then, after Co-Co died, we adopted two new Maine Coons that we named Marnie and Molly. When Wally disappeared, I felt the need to adopt again and got a black and white cat from the NHSPCA. We called him Hoover "the Huv." We later added a Maine Coon named Chester and Clay's beloved cat, Porter. Porter was a stray who Clay first started feeding, then let live in the yard, then to the horror of Hoover, let into the house. Eventually, Porter got bold enough to sleep with Clay. The two had a special bond that lasted all their lives. When Clay was first in the hospital, all he worried about was Porter —

Clay and Wahl and Verne

The Wahl

was he okay? Would he remember him when he came home? When Clay did return home, Porter came right to him and got in his lap. Clay just cried and cried. During Clay's last illness, Porter passed while Clay was sick. However, I think he was waiting for Clay to join him and I have no doubt that they are together now.

All of our cats are buried in our garden. When Clay and I moved to Portsmouth, we had the ashes of all but three of our cats with us. We felt like Portsmouth would be our final home, and so we took the ashes to a lovely spot in the garden, mixed them together and buried them. In this way, all of our beloved pets are with us always.

The orange and black kitties are my current kitties Lucy and Henrietta. Lucy is the "kleptomaniac cat," as she likes to "borrow" things from guests.

Lucy loves sleeping with AirBNB guests.

The Huv (Hoover) sleeping

*Ruth's goodbye
to Hoover*

*Ruth getting her hair
washed by Henrietta*

Today I have Sir Ashley Wilcox Stump, a large, gray and white cat who reminds me of Clay. Sometimes I feel Clay's spirit is in him somehow. He follows me about and sleeps with me, and just seems to be taking care of me in some fashion. I also have Henrietta, a beautiful all black cat, and Lucy, a female orange tiger from Puerto Rico. She lived on the streets and is a bit of a kleptomaniac, as guests have reported her going off with various items when they have stayed here. These cats are my family and great company. They have their own stories which I will tell one day.

Of course, our cats are well known around the neighborhood. They can frequently be seen sitting on our front step, and often neighbors, or complete strangers, will open the door to let them in!

"Eau Claire"

College gang in Eau Claire

The Barracuda in a car show

CHAPTER FIVE:
OFF TO EAU CLAIRE: 1973-1980

The house in Eau Claire started a whole new chapter in our lives. Despite the traumatic beginning, it was a time that was mostly happy and would turn out to be a new start for me. We got to our new home on December 28, 1973. By the time the moving van arrived on December 31st, I had all the wallpaper removed from the dining room and music room and all the woodwork painted. Clay thought I moved along pretty fast on the house in Columbus, but soon realized I'd been working in slow motion compared to our house in Eau Claire.

I found a job in the local hospital working as a private secretary to the head of maintenance, a position that had always been held by a female. I worked there for three years and loved it; the staff loved Clay too, regardless of our lifestyle. His breadmaking won their stomachs and hearts. After three years, my employers tried to transfer me to the mail room because of seniority issues. I refused to go and quit. Oops — bad decision as that meant no unemployment check and thus no income.

I had a friend who owned a paint store. I had pretty much helped keep them in business as we now had two houses and with all the renovating, I had been buying paint by the bucketful. He hired me for three months and then laid me off, which meant the hospital had to pay my unemployment. Smart move, Verne!

The summer of 1976 brought more emotional upheaval due to my mother. Evelyn came to visit after her first cancer operation, on July 4, 1974. She and I had fun the first few days, but on the fourth or fifth day she started in on me. "You don't appreciate Clay. You let him do all the work. You don't deserve him."

Finally I sat her down on the front porch and told her to keep her mouth shut until I was finished talking. She did for a change. I told her she was a guest in our house, eating our food, drinking our booze, playing our piano, driving one of our cars. If she didn't like what she saw, she was free to leave at any time. I told her that we would drive her to the airport and pay for her airfare. My speaking up like that brought her up short. She stopped harping at me and wound up staying for not only the planned two weeks, but another week as well. It was the best and last fun we had with her, as she died of cancer not long after.

The last two years of my mom's life were terrible to watch. She had another operation, more chemotherapy, and radiation. By the time she died, she weighed less than 50 pounds, had lost all of her beautiful hair, and was unable to show anything but hate for me. Before she died, I had been trying to hold onto my job at the hospital but had to travel home twice during her last two months.

The first trip was to help her pack and the second was to take her to buy new furniture and move her into a new apartment. She thought that if she bought new furniture, God would let her live. I knew time was getting short, and after I lost my job, I went to stay with her. Despite the horrible way she had treated me, I guess I still hoped for some closure, some healing.

After all, she was my mother. But no redemption ever came — just more pain. A few months before she passed, she had asked my sister, brother and me to tell her what we wanted. The only things I wanted were those items that had belonged to my beloved Mom-Mom. Instead, my mother gave everything I requested to my siblings. My sister admitted that my mother even made them promise not to give me anything I wanted — she hated my lifestyle that much. I did get a few pieces later on, including Mom-Mom's rocker, but most items were kept from me. For the last 35 years of

Verne's grandparents' and mother's family plot

his life, my brother would not speak to me and I never found out why. He stopped speaking to me right after our father died; both his wife and my sister claimed to not know why. Not long before he died, my sister felt that he was rethinking his feelings toward me and wanted to reconnect but didn't know how, but he died before he could reach out. I always wondered if my mother had said something to him to turn him against me, but I never knew for sure. It became just another painful chapter in my family history.

After my mother died, Clay and I still faced the problem of a reduced income. It was obvious that I needed to find a viable career. We had enough to pay all of our bills with the exception of the mortgages. It was also obvious that I was unhappy. Clay enjoyed his academic career, but I hated being in the position of "faculty wife." One night at dinner, we were having drinks and I was telling him how miserable I was and grousing about being unemployed. After heavy discussion (which in some circles might be described as arguments), Clay said, "Verne, what do you want to be when you grow up?" He knew I needed a sense of direction. I said, "An interior designer" and he immediately said, "Then let's do it!" We finally agreed that I should enroll at the University of Wisconsin at Menomonee in their new art program. Bam! I was off and running. I graduated cum laude three years later with a major in Interior Design.

With the family drama behind me, and a new career about to launch, life should have been smooth sailing, but that was not the case. So much happened while we lived in Eau Claire. Some things showed a side of me that only Clay's love could see through. That love kept me on course and eventually helped me be the person Clay believed I could be.

I had met Dale before I started school. Dale was very beautiful, twenty years old, and very confused about his sexuality. Meeting me allowed him to be who he really was. We fell madly in love. I still loved Clay, but my feelings for Dale were strong, though different. When we met, he was living in Eau Claire, but he soon found a room in Minneapolis. In fact, Clay and I helped him move

Dale

there. For over a year, I spent most of my weekends in Minneapolis with Dale. Sometime Clay and I would both go and we would all party together, hitting up the gay bars until the wee hours of the mornings. It was, after all, the "Gay 90s" (more on this later on). Clay knew of my affair, but it is a measure of his character, and his deep love for me, that he did not let it come between us. He could have kicked me out and been justified, but he believed so strongly in our relationship, that he decided to wait it out. With my history, he knew that being in a long-term, committed relationship was new to me. He understood that part of me still couldn't believe that someone could love me forever.

My relationship with Dale came to an abrupt end on a snowy

Saturday night when I woke up at 1:00 a.m. and found Dale in bed with three other men. We had been sleeping in the guest room; I awoke and found he was not beside me. I went to the master bedroom, and there he was having sex with those men. I dressed, got in my car, and drove home through the blinding snow, crying all the way. It was three o'clock in the morning when I pulled into our driveway in Eau Claire. Clay had locked the door as he typically did at night. Still crying, I banged on the door until Clay, clad in his pajamas, came down and let me in. When he opened the door, he simply took me in his arms and started to cry as well. I said "I'm back, love," and he said, "I knew you would be." Despite all the drama, Dale remained in our lives as a friend and we kept in touch even after we moved to Boston.

The episode with Dale was probably the most trying time in our 46 years together. During that year, Clay showed me how much he truly loved me. Even though it hurt him deeply, he gave me the respect and time to work myself through my relationship with Dale. Such love as Clay gave me I knew I didn't deserve — I thought that then, and I think that now, but I am so glad that he let me figure things out on my own. That allowed me to grow. All Clay needed to have said was, "Him or me, but not both ways," and I probably would have ended it with Dale sooner. But his acceptance of my feelings for Dale showed me what true love was all about. I'm still learning about this even now. I feel that Clay and I grew more, learned more about ourselves, and learned more about each other in Eau Claire than during any other period of our life together.

During those first years in Eau Claire, I had convinced myself that I hated the place and made college a way to escape. When I look back, I remember how much fun we had and think of all the many dear friends we made. We were wise enough to rent out our spare bedroom, and so a succession of young men moved in. Most of them became good friends — some to this day. Among our renters were, Dave, who had been a roommate of Tom's, my business partner. I had started an interior design business when I started college, assisting clients here and there. As the business progressed, I did more and more of the design and Tom primarily did the labor. Don, another art student lived next to us. Dave and Don introduced us to many more friends and fun times. Most of our friends were faculty members from one school or another, and interestingly, most were straight.

Among the more memorable escapades we had was a camping trip we took with Dave, Suzie, Dave's girlfriend, and Don. We arrived at this very redneck campground in the red Barracuda in the pouring rain. Clay, myself and Don were in one tent with Dave and Suzie in the other. It was challenging to say the least to get the tents up in what seemed like a monsoon.

We went next door to visit Suzie and Dave, and Suzie made us take our shoes off because she had a clean white blanket on the floor. Once in, we opened some wine. I started to lean against a pole and the entire tent collapsed onto the clean white floor. I put the tent back up and returned to ours, never to be invited back.

That night, we had reservations at a very fine restaurant in the area and had planned to dress for the occasion. Despite the weather, and to the amazement of our fellow campers, we emerged from our tents in formal attire — Suzie in a long dress and heels and the rest of us in suits and ties. I think the folks at the campground must have talked about that for years. In those years, it seemed that we left behind some kind of an impression no matter where we went. I like to think that people still laugh or smile, even now, when they remember us. These memories and laughs keep me going.

Ah, the parties! I can't talk about Eau Claire without mentioning the parties. We had entertaining down to an art. Clay was in the kitchen and I handled the front of house, and what a house it was! We usually had friends over for drinks and dinner once or twice a month. We had a wonderful front porch; it was a three-season porch that could be entered from both the living and dining rooms. It was a superb place to entertain and entertain we did.

I won't try to remember all of our parties, but I am going to recall a few that were the most fun. I was enrolled in the art department at the University of Wisconsin/Stout and one of our renters, Don, was enrolled at the University of Wisconsin/Eau Claire where Clay taught. Don and I were always at odds as to which school had the best art program. I decided to have a very large party and invite the faculty from both schools' art programs. The party was a huge success and really brought people together.

To this day, 36 years later, both art programs still work together for the betterment of their students. I know this because I have been back twice and the faculty still talks about that party.

The next to last party we had in Eau Claire was our annual Christmas party, and it was memorable. The Christmas party was typically large — faculty and friends from both schools, our renters and their friends (we now owned the house next door), and our neighbors. One of our guests was Dale, my ex-lover, who now lived in the Twin Cities.

Among the guests was a couple we'd known for years and who came to all of our parties. He was a closet queen (meaning he was gay but not out; however, everyone knew he was gay, as he was frequently spotted cruising around town, but his wife claimed not to know). During the course of the party, she discovered her husband and Dale on top of the guest coats on our bed almost naked, having sex. She started screeching and cussing and we could hear the noise downstairs. Some of the other guests and I ran up to our bedroom, where we found the two men frantically trying to pull their pants up and the wife standing and screaming with a drink in her hand. When she saw me she shrieked, "How dare you have this whore in Clay's house!" She slapped me across the face — twice — then threw her drink in my face. The cool ice felt good on my hot stinging cheek, but as for the drink, I never did like gin. They left; Dale stayed and the party began...

Our last year in Eau Claire was bittersweet for both of us. Clay was at the university with tenure and very comfortable. I had fallen in step with him, and we both felt settled. Clay's support had helped me realize that I had a brain, I had talent, I wasn't just a "fluff" person or partier. Thanks to his encouragement, and the fact that I earned scholarships and got good grades, I felt like I was making something of myself. This feeling was brought home in one special moment during the holidays. For a friend's Christmas party that last year, Clay helped me pick out a new, three-piece, pinstriped suit. He was wearing a beautiful herringbone sport jacket that he had inherited from his father and a spiffy bow tie. I sometimes tended to get a little chubby, but had lost a lot of weight during my three years in school. When we walked into the party we both knew that we looked "hot." A queen who had wanted to bed Clay down for years walked up to him and said, "I see you have a cute new boyfriend. What happened to Verne?" Clay put his arm around me, kissed me on the cheek, and said, "This is my Verne!" We were so proud of who we were and what we had accomplished in Eau Claire. While writing it down and remembering, I think that night was one of the most precious moments in all of our 45 years together.

My final semester in college was rough on both of us. I had, somehow, maintained a 4.0 average for the entire time I'd been there, but realized I would not reach that level in the last semester (I knew I had one B and maybe even a C coming). Frustrated, I decided to just kick back, let the old Verne take over, and party. (Despite my self-destructive tendencies, I did manage to graduate cum laude.)

Just before finals, my "college gang," Randy, Brad, Diane, and John invited me out for drinks. We were at the bar when Diane said, "Call Clay and get him to come over; we can all go do dinner." I got hold of Clay as he was leaving the university and after much chanting by the group — "Come on, Clay! Come on, Clay!" — he agreed to come.

We never left the bar. We drank there; we ate there; we drank there. Around 11:00 p.m., Clay announced to the group that he was going home (a distance of 38 miles) and that I should leave as well. Clay had the red Barracuda, which had a bad muffler and was very loud. Having had less to drink, he said that he would take that car and let me bring the BYB (big yellow Buick). He did not want to risk me getting pulled over for a loud muffler. Well, I didn't exactly leave right after Clay as planned. I left the bar after last call at 1:00 a.m. Unfortunately, the BYB had a burnt out low beam on the driver's side.

Diane asked me if I would drive her home because she was too drunk to walk, and of course I said 'yes.' After I dropped her off, I saw a cop approaching me. I knew if I dimmed my lights he would stop me, so I did not lower them; however, he stopped me for not dimming them! When he came to speak with me, he then found I'd been drinking. Back at the police station, I was allowed one phone call and whom did I call? Diane. The police wound up calling Clay, which scared him to death, as he was sure I'd had an accident. When he arrived at the station at 1:30 a.m., he was not a happy camper.

For starters, he had to pay my fine, since I'd spent all my money at the bar. I had been warned that if I drove again that morning and got stopped, I would face jail time, but Clay had no choice but to let me drive, because we each needed a car in the morning. I promised Clay that I'd follow him home, but about halfway there, I passed him and started to speed up. Clay immediately pulled over and turned off his lights. I know when I'm beat, so I pulled over and turned off my lights as well. Clay pulled up beside me with the dome light on and screamed, "I told you to follow me." I was laughing. Clay was not.

The last two months were the most stressful for both of us. Clay decided that he wanted to stay on at the university for another year, while I had made up my mind that I was leaving the University and Eau Claire after our tenth anniversary on May 15th. Where I was headed, I didn't know — I just wanted out of Eau Claire and academia. Maybe New Orleans. We went into my last week before graduation talking about how to break up the house and all of our belongings — even our precious cats.

I wanted nothing but a few pieces of art and Mom-Mom's rocker. I'm finding it hard, even now, to remember this time and write about it. I was in the studio, making my presentation to the class, when Kathy, the department chair, came into the studio and said to me,

"Verne, you need to come into my office. Clay's on the phone." I told her to tell him I'd call back after my presentation. She said, "Now, Verne. He's crying."

I went to the office and picked up the phone. Through sobs, Clay said, "How about Boston?" By now, I was crying as well. I said, "Yes!" And so we began the next 18 years.

The last party lasted for days. It started with my graduation on the 10th and continued until we celebrated our anniversary on the 15th. It was a small group, and my sister, Tippy, came up from West Virginia, which made it special. We then packed the U-haul with our most prized possessions including art. After staging both houses to show, as they would be going up for sale, Tip and I headed east. We were pulling the U-haul with the BYB and journeying to Tippy's home, then I would head north. Clay had to stay behind to finish grading finals. He later came east with a friend who was going to Hartford to visit her daughter. I hooked up with him in Harrisburg and we headed for Boston.

As I look back, I realize that neither of us should have gone through the trauma of that near breakup. If Clay had dug in his heels and decided he was not leaving Eau Claire, we were enough in step with one another that I would have stayed. Deep down, I knew that being with him was more important than the geographical place we were in. I was always restless, but Clay had become a constant in my life, and one that I could not live with out.

Clay and Verne
in the Eau Claire dining room

"Dear Friends"

Mike

Tom,
lost but not to Aids

Paul

San Francisco

CHAPTER SIX:
THE AIDS CRISIS

Thoughts of the Aids Crisis still stir up so many emotions. We met many of our dearest friends during our Columbus years and too many of them passed away from Aids. Mike was Clay's ex-lover when we met; Glen had been my friend, lover and roommate until I met Clay and was forever after a member of our family. "Long Tall Paul" was another dear friend — he took his last vacation with us before he died in 1979. Then there were the three crazy Jerries who spent vacations with us in Provincetown in the early eighties. It is hard to believe that they are all gone.

Dear Mike was a party type of guy who would go to Provincetown with us and then be gone all night having sex under the docks. He'd come in the following morning exhausted but happy. I never told Clay, because I knew it would upset him, but, the last time we visited Mike and his new lover in Cleveland, Mike and I had a poignant conversation. We knew Mike was very ill; he only weighed 90 lbs. and was very, very weak. I awoke in the middle of the night to go to the bathroom and found him sitting in the living room with his head in his hands, sobbing like a baby. I sat next to him, pulled him close and asked what was wrong? He hugged me and said, "Verne, I've looked all my life for someone to love me the way Clay loves you. I finally found him and now I'm dying. Why Verne, Why?" I didn't have an answer; I just laid down with him and cried. We stayed that way until dawn. Clay and I left the next day and he died the next week.

Long Tall Paul, so called because he was tall and very skinny, went with us to London in 1982. What fun we had! We stayed in a steel city north of London called Bradford. One of Clay's fellow cooking school students owned a house there and let us use it for two weeks. Bradford was a blue-collar town and the neighbors didn't know what to make of the three queens next door. We didn't care. We had candlelight dinners every night, took long day trips to Scotland and Wales, and Paul went wading in the North Sea. It was amazing. I never told Clay, but when we met Paul at his house in Columbus, I saw the medications he took. He had a full knapsack of pills and liquids. I got the feeling then that our dear friend had Aids. Three months after we got home from England, Paul died of pneumonia. He was the first of our family (all of our gay friends were considered family) to be lost to Aids and so the horror of that word entered our lives.

Then there was our Glen. The dearest, sweetest, craziest man we knew. We last saw him at his mother's farm in Kentucky in 1989. When we had our all-night talk, he said that he wasn't sorry about dying. In fact, he said, "Verne, it's been a fun life and you and Clay were a large part of it." He was already having memory problems and asked me to write a letter telling him about the Columbus years and some of our experiences. He wanted to remember them before he died. When we got home, I composed his letter but his mother did not have Internet so I had to mail it. He died before the letter reached him but his mother got it. I'm going to share a bit of our time with Glen here — a tribute to one of so many dear friends lost.

I met Glen in the summer of 1967. I was in Columbus, Ohio and was 27. I had been divorced for three years. I had just survived my first gay relationship and was footloose and fancy free. I was friends with the three Jerrys, Long Tall Paul, John and Bob. They were a few years younger than me and we all hung out on weekends at the Cat's Meow, the gay bar behind the railway station. Glen appeared one Friday night and we started dishing each other at once. I remember Bob saying, "Oh shit, here we go." We both knew from the get-go that we were sisters. Glen was soon part of the group. We all spent every weekend either there or across town at another bar that was more upscale — the beer cost more and you couldn't dance. But, no matter where we went, we'd check out the men and carry on like "White Trash" — generally doing a lot of whoring around. Some nights we scored but most nights we just had fun.

We talked on the phone a lot — about who we thought was cute, who we thought was nerdy, who we wanted to sleep with and who we didn't, who we thought was sleeping with whom and why. Girl talk!

I took Glen to Belle Vernon to meet my mom and my sister, Tippy. She was home from design school in West Virginia. She thought Glen was a little weird but I told her she was wrong — Glen was a lot weird! He kept popping up unexpectedly during the week — at Bob's, my place, John's place, and was always saying, "Turn the hot water on, I need my tea!" One day I got a phone call from Tippy, who was living on a farm in Bull's Creek Holler. She said, "You'll never guess who's sitting on my front porch — it's Glen!" She said he had a cup of tea, took a nap, and left. A little weird? A lot weird!

We visited Glen in the summer of 1986 and had a blast going to the gay rodeo. By now the Aids Crisis was in full cry. Glen never told us what he was really going through. The next time I visited, I came by myself — I think it, was a business trip — and it was then that I realized how sick Glen was. I had made plans to fly up to San Francisco and Glen wanted to go there one more time. He knew that he would then have to go back home to Kentucky because he could no longer live by himself — he was very, very weak.

We rented a car and drove up. It took two days because Glen couldn't sit for long periods of time. When we got there, I didn't tell Glen then, but I called my friend Roberta. I told her that I was with Glen and he was ill. She asked me what he had and I told her

AIDS. She said I could not bring him anywhere near her. So we stayed at a hotel for two days before I put Glen on the plane back home. I always suspected he knew Roberta would not let us come see her.

I returned home with a heavy heart but Clay and I made up our minds to do whatever we could to help Glen. So when he called us a month later to tell us he was in Kentucky, we had to see him. He was very weak, but still very much crazy Glen.

I remember Glen and I lying on his mother's sofa. His head was in my lap and he was looking up at the ceiling. He started to laugh and I said, "What ya laughing at girl?" He said, "They're so funny, and you can't even see them! There's creepy-crawlies all over the ceiling." Glen started to cry and told me he loved me. He said that he was ready to give up. We talked about the new drugs that were coming out every week and that (at that time) our mutual friend Long Tall Paul was holding his own. I told him that, yes, we had lost a great many friends to this terrible disease but there was always hope, always hope, always hope!

When we left Glen the next day, he said that he would do what the doctor and his mother told him to do and would try to get his strength up. Still, it was a very sad drive home. A few weeks later, his mother called. Glen had died. They buried him on the hill overlooking his house. I said, "Keep the water hot, Glen; we'll catch up soon."

Clay and I both feared that, because of my sleeping around with other men, that I or both of us probably had Aids. We were afraid to be tested. During this time, I actually tried to push Clay away because I loved him so much and was so afraid of giving him Aids. I had told him when we first met that I never wanted him to tell me that he loved me or I'd leave him. I didn't want that responsibility. I had never been treated like I was worthy of being loved—not by my parents, not by anyone—so I just lived like today was my last. I think deep down I really believed I did not deserve love. I felt sooner or later that Clay would see the real Verne and get tired of him and go, so I kept that wall up. I wasn't going to let love in. I couldn't handle it. I was afraid of it and the Aids Crisis intensified that fear.

Initially, we thought Aids was caused by using Poppers (an inhaled recreational drug) during sex and while dancing, so everybody stopped using Poppers but the deaths kept happening. Mostly it was our younger friends who were succumbing so that made it doubly sad.

Why were the 1990s referred to by gay culture as the "Gay 90s"? I can only answer for myself, and I think for Clay, too, but I would say that it was because we finally had a presidential leader, Bill Clinton, who was young and dynamic. We felt that he would get things done and bring about positive change. Clinton also had a partner who stuck by him, no matter what — that showed us that we could have happy, long-term relationships as well. He might have been the president, but he was also a human being with very human flaws and those didn't impair his ability to lead. Whatever the reason, the nineties became a time when gay culture was galvanized into action — when our needs and issues were brought to the forefront. Gay people became a vital and vocal part of the population and roared into life.

I think this decade was also transforming because we gays had gone through a very dark period the decade before thanks to the arrival of the Aids Crisis. The "brand" we had been forced to wear had been lifted. It came to light that Aids wasn't just a "gay disease that God cast down" to punish us, but a virus that could afflict the heterosexual population as well. A burden was lifted. We had suffered the great loss of so many of our culture during the initial years of the Crisis, but now, this situation was getting better thanks to the discovery of the "Aids cocktail," a combination of drugs that were supposed to put the disease into remission. We relaxed a bit because we knew that sex wasn't going to kill us and we could have it again if we wanted to. Think about it — making love is one of life's most basic acts and most compelling needs, yet we as a culture avoided engaging in sex for fear we would die or that we would unwittingly transfer the disease to those we cared for and then they would die. That fear traumatized you mind, body and soul. For those of us who were young and carefree in our sex lives in the seventies and eighties, it was like living with a time bomb ticking every day. Would one night's pleasure wind up killing you? None of us knew.

Sadly, I could go on and on about the impact of Aids on our lives. We lost at least eight of our 12 best friends in one decade. Sometimes it seemed like all we did was attend funerals. They were all young, beautiful men, and at that time, the world didn't care that they were dying. Some even thought it was justified, a scourge put upon us for being gay, for being who we were. Clay and I were lucky to have survived but the Aids Crisis was forever seared into our hearts.

The boys from Columbus —
Verne is the only one still alive.

Boys in the Barracuda

Clay and Glen

"Parties and Friends"

Clay in costume

*Clay, Marnie, and Verne
at National Day community
celebration in Boston*

CHAPTER SEVEN:
BOSTON
WEST SPRINGFIELD STREET
1980-1981

We arrived in Boston on May 29th. The city was alive with celebration—it was Boston's 350th anniversary and Memorial Day weekend. We stayed the first night at a rundown hotel in Brighton and then the next few nights at Copley Place, which was next to the Hancock Tower. This would have been more spectacular except the tower was covered in plywood. A design flaw was causing the glass in the windows to suddenly pop out and fall to the street!

On Memorial Day we all but skipped as we walked along, holding hands. We strolled by the Charles River, crossed the bridge into Cambridge, and had dinner at the top of the Hyatt. What a wonderful day we had. For the next four days, we explored the city together. We dined at the Seaside and Cityside restaurants at Faneuil Hall, the wonderful German restaurant in the Crescent Building and at Lock-Obers. We went to the bars Clay had visited when he attended dance workshops many years ago. On our last night together, Clay took me to Napoleon's, a gay bar. He took a note off the board that read, "Roommate wanted. Call # and ask for xxxxxxx." Due to Boston's high rental costs, I would need a roommate until Clay came back East in the fall. The next day, he went back to Eau Claire to teach summer school and sell the houses.

Thus my first summer in Boston started with me living with "Ask for." Now, "Ask for" had a beautiful ranch-style home in the 'burbs with a two-car garage and a completely furnished apartment in the basement. My room, if I decided to take it, was the master bedroom with private bath; "Ask for" agreed to take the guest room. I moved in, although I already knew I should have said, "No thanks." Clay agreed that I should have said "no thanks," but it was too late. I then started looking for a job. No problem, I thought, me having that "cum laude" and all.

It turned out finding a job was a big problem. Wherever I went, I struck out. I was quickly hit with the reality that there were no jobs. Still, I managed to meet interesting people at the bars, and one I met soon became a friend. Ron was involved with a local theater group, and they hired me to design the set for a play they were doing. This was not exactly what I had in mind for work but it was fun and I met some likable people.

That 4th of July was one I will never forget. Seeing the Hatch Shell, the Boston Pops, and thousands of people streaming into Boston was incredible. I couldn't wait to call Clay in the morning, I was so excited.

My summer with "Ask for" was also wild and crazy. "Ask for" worked as a public servant.

Every week, Monday through Wednesday, without fail all I heard was, "I'm never gonna have another drink." Thursday through Sunday was a different story. He drank so much my guess is that he used a funnel. This went on every week for the entire summer.

"Ask for" took a real liking to me. (I may have encouraged it a wee bit.) Clay arrived in mid-August in the red Barracuda with a car full of our five cats, plants and a U-haul packed with furniture. I had been waiting for him to help me find an apartment for us. Hearing this, "Ask for" came up with a wonderful plan for his apartment in the basement. We could move in, rent-free. Clay could cook for us all; we would share the grocery bill—and Clay would share me. I thought it might work but Clay strongly disagreed. Ultimately, we found an apartment and were moved in by September 1st. Thank God we found a landlord who liked cats!

Verne, Kurt and Clay

But before I move on with our story, I have to back up to "Ask for." The one thing he gave us was Kurt. We met Kurt at the first and last Xmas party "Ask for" ever had on December 28, 1980. He was a wonderful artist and I have several pieces of his work. Kurt was a big part of our lives ever since that crazy summer and a very large part of mine until this year. I went to visit him and celebrate my birthday, as I've done every year since Clay died. He got very drunk and at 1:00 a.m. on the morning of my birthday, burst into my room and started punching me. I had been asleep until he attacked. He was screaming that he was bi-polar and going crazy and he wanted me to get out of his apartment and go home.

This tirade went on until 3:00 a.m. when he went to bed. At 5:00 a.m. I got up, dressed and went to the airport. I caught a flight for home, still shaken by what had happened. That was the end of Kurt in my life. There had been glimpses before that incident that Kurt had an illness, but I had not seen any real signs, only heard of these issues from friends. Evidently, his continued alcohol abuse pushed him over the edge. I understand that he is now in a relationship with someone who is keeping an eye on him, but that his behavior can still be erratic. The whole birthday episode was so sad. I really loved him and still think of him every time I look at a piece of his art.

The new apartment was on West Springfield Street in the South End. It was unique and very beautiful, but as it turned out, we had a very bad year there. Maybe its odd features should have tipped us off. The walls of the West Springfield home were strange. Both floors had exposed brick on one side. All of the art that we hung on the brick walls would get about two inches of water in the bottom of the frames. This was both bizarre and disturbing as all of our art was original pieces. Where was the water coming from? We didn't find out until after we moved. The City started working on the street and discovered there was a leak in the water supply to our building and that leak fed into the walls of our apartment.

Our first and only Christmas there was a blast. The unit was very contemporary in feel so our black ebony Victorian parlor and dining sets didn't work. I put the furniture in storage in "Ask for's" garage and headed off to Bloomingdales. Ten thousand dollars later, we had furniture that fit the apartment. Mind you neither Clay nor I had found a job yet. By the time we did, we had only $250 left in the bank out of the $53,000 we had cleared on the sale of the two houses.

As a result, that first Christmas was on the slim. The unit consisted of two floors, the basement and sub-basement.. The lower floor had the kitchen in the back (street side), then the living floor, which extended beyond the bedroom floor above. The master bedroom had a balcony that allowed you to look down onto the living room and the fireplace. The living room had glass sliders onto a small patio at the rear of the house.

For Christmas, we bought a 15-foot tree that extended from the living area, up past the bedroom balcony. I had been telling all of our new friends that we had accumulated many beautiful tree decorations in our 10 years together, and we invited everyone for a mulled wine and tree trimming party. With great fanfare, and with champagne in hand, we opened the boxes of decorations only to discover that we had mistakenly brought the stuff we wanted to throw away, and had left the good stuff in the attic in Eau Clair. Party over. All went home. Naked tree!

The problem was solved the next week by our artsy new friend Ron, who brought yards and yards of pink velvet ribbon and buckets of fake snow for another attempt at a tree trimming party. Everybody stood on the balcony in the bedroom and threw handfuls of snow at the tree; we then went downstairs and tied pink velvet ribbons on all the branches. Clay and I had already purchased our traditional decoration for the season, a small glass pregnant pussy, which we hung on the most piss-elegant tree I've ever seen. We hung that pussy on every tree we ever had, and I still display her each year.

Pregnant pussy ornament

That year, we hosted the Christmas party for the architectural firm where I had found a job. Anatol, our graphic designer, walked through the unopened sliding glass doors with a drink in his hand and never spilled a drop. Russians know how to hold their vodka.

The bad luck we had with the apartment occurred early on. We were broken into twice in the first month, losing all of Clay's grandmother's pearl-handled sterling silver and all of our jewelry, except what we were wearing. I happened to be wearing Clay's father's antique ring or that would have been taken as well. That night, through tears. Clay said to me, "Verne, that ring is forever yours. You saved it." I've worn it every day since. Burglars broke in again a year later just as we were ready to sign the lease for our second year. After that we decided to move on.

As it turned out, I thought that the break ins were one of the best things that could have happened to us as they spurred us to find a new home. We never would have lived in such an incredible spot if we had stayed in West Springfield. Clay never quite agreed.

Our life-changing move came about just as I had joined the staff working for Michael Dukakis's second run for governor. That very morning I had called about an apartment on Beacon Street. It was across from the Public Garden, in one of the original brownstones. It was literally two doors down from the "Cheers," bar made famous by the popular television show.

Clay and I met up after my meeting with Dukakis, so we were both dressed in suits and ties. The landlord was very impressed with us and took us through one of the most elegant apartments I had ever seen. He rented it to us that night. I remember going into the Public Garden, looking at the building and saying to myself, "Verne, you must be dreaming. How could this happen?"

CHAPTER EIGHT:
WE HAVE ARRIVED!
BOSTON:
BEACON STREET   1981-1997

When we moved in, I finally realized that we had entered another phase in our lives. We were in Boston for over eight years. For me, they were the most fun-filled years of my life, although I realize now that they were not always that much fun for Clay.

The day we moved in, Clay's dear friend, Mike, came to visit. We left everything in the middle of the floor and left the next day for Provincetown for two weeks. That trip was especially memorable because we got ourselves escorted out of P-Town by the sheriff. When we were getting ready to leave, I had pulled my car up outside the inn so we could more easily load. A rather loud-mouthed neighbor evidently thought we were taking too long and started heckling us. I'd finally had enough and told him to fuck himself. He took offense and called the police. When the cop arrived, he took the neighbor's side. He asked us if we had everything, then said he would escort us out of town. He even sat and waited to make sure we left. In fact, he warned us that if we circled back into town for anything he would have us arrested. Thus ended our trip to Provincetown!

When we got home, for me, the fun started. Our grand five-story building faced Beacon Street. Our apartment was on the third floor of the back part of the house; this was actually the top floor as the back of the house had fewer stories than the front. The second floor would have been the formal dining room and there was also a richly paneled library. The first floor was where the kitchen would have been. What a grand space our apartment was! Upon opening the front door one looked through our living room with its 15-foot ceiling and fireplace; you also glimpsed the dining room (with a 12-foot ceiling) and the den/kitchen area (eight-foot ceilings). If the rooms weren't dazzling enough, a mirrored wall reflected everything back. To top things off, there was a skylight above the mirror. Everything seemed to gleam!

Behind all the gleam was our tiny bedroom which shared the wonderful skylight. The view out our bedroom windows included the CITGO sign at the Red Sox stadium, the Charles River and Cambridge. Out of our large windows, we could watch the crowds crossing the Arthur Fiedler footbridge; we could see over to Storrow Drive and the Hatch Shell, view the Community Boating boats bobbing in the river and enjoy the lights of Cambridge beyond.

It was a great space, inside and out. I remember us sitting on the front steps watching the couples strolling in the Public Garden across the street. Kevin White, who was mayor of Boston for years, would occasionally walk by in the evening. He would often sit down and talk with us. He was a great storyteller, and always had a joke for Clay, which Clay then had to explain to me later. He loved Clay's sense of humor.

Whether you entered or exited our building, it was always a visually striking experience. Coming out of those great old double

Beacon Street

*Arthur Fiedler
Footbridge*

*View from
bedroom window*

doors in the evening after a snowfall always took our breath away. Seeing the Public Garden in summer was equally lovely. Entering the house brought you into a white marble foyer with a curved, white marble staircase. The staircase went all the way to the third floor. There was also an old dumbwaiter that went from the basement, which had housed the original kitchen, to the floor above us, which would have been the nursery. The dumbwaiter was now a one-person elevator. For some reason, our unit was still labeled "Aunt Bertha's bedroom suite"—we often chuckled about that!

I had so much fun in Boston, but Clay did not. Looking back now, I realize that it was because he was watching me start to self-destruct and didn't know how to stop it. We partied; we spent excessively; we vacationed; we lived always for today and never worried about tomorrow. I was always saying, "Don't worry about money, Clay, I'll take care of it"—except I couldn't. During this period, I had to declare bankruptcy twice and made Clay do it once. He was so ashamed. We even bought two antique Mercedes with credit cards. Clay let me bottom out again and again, but always picked up the pieces. I was his Humpty Dumpty.

Part of our financial crisis stemmed from the fact that a few weeks after we got back from Provincetown, the firm where I was employed collapsed. We had only Clay's income. Fortunately, my firm had several clients who liked my work, so I found myself being hired to freelance.

One of these firms was the United States Air Force at Pease Air Force Base; this was located an hour north of Boston in Portsmouth, New Hampshire. This is how we found Portsmouth and fell in love with the city, although we would not move there for several more years. By this time, we had taken an extra room on the third floor of the Beacon Street apartment; it had once been a maid's room but became my office. Clay was very pleased to have me out of his kitchen.

When we moved into Beacon Street, I realized that we had entered another phase in our lives. The first party at 93 was our second annual Halloween party in Boston. It was a little rowdier than the first one in West Springfield, and there was no glass door for Anatol to walk through. Even though my firm had already shut down and money was tight, we still wanted to party and did we ever!

We had a New Year's Eve party that year which was wonderful, but then came the 4th of July. Wow, friends came out of the woodwork! Location, location, location. This was the first of eight 4th of July's at 93 Beacon Street. Each one got bigger and better. In fact, all of our parties got bigger and better during those eight years. As I said — location, location, location.

After the first four years, Clay quit trying to do all the cooking and we had them catered. This eased the stress but upped the cost. We had over 200 people at some of the parties; the 4th of July's and Halloweens were the largest.

For Halloween, Clay and I had an unspoken agreement that neither of us would wear a costume. I would have loved one, but Clay was more reserved. He liked to watch other people have fun but sometimes found it hard to let go and have fun himself. I also think that he trusted me more in terms of my not getting into trouble when he could keep an eye on me! For three years, I kept this promise, but then came year four. For some reason, I got this wild hair up my butt. The day before the party, I rented a costume. The only thing that fit me was a Catholic cardinal's red peaked cap and gown. I then bought a full face mask, shoes, socks, and the most god-awful plastic ring I could find. I stored all this in the gold Mercedes which was parked down on the street.

About halfway through the party, I sneaked out and changed into my costume in the gold Mercedes. As I was coming back in the front door at 93 Beacon, a couple came in with me; they were dressed as a priest and a pregnant nun and they were coming to our party. I recognized them as our landlord and his girlfriend, but they had no idea who I was. I stayed a mystery guest until almost the end of the party. Every time I passed Clay, I thrust that god-awful ring in his face and he kissed it. Suddenly, Joyce, a close friend, came up to me and said, "Who are you?" She looked closely into my eyes, saw the intense blue, and said, "My God, it's Verne!" I don't think Clay ever forgave me. If he did, he never told me. He never liked being played for a fool.

Despite all the parties, and our lovely home, these were tough times for Clay. He had finished school at Newberry College with yet another degree. This one was in culinary arts. This change was initially a hard one. Clay had gotten his Ph.D. in Audiology and loved helping people. When we first came to Boston, he was working in the Audiology Department at Boston University, but after his first year, his boss told me that he was not renewing Clay's contract.

He knew Clay loved to cook and was good at it, and asked me to encourage Clay to go to culinary school. I did, and Clay took the advice, but deep down, he still missed working in his field. Clay eventually started working for a woman named Ellen, who did catering for large functions such as wedding dinners and receptions, many featuring lobster bakes and such. It was a lot of work on nights and weekends. I sometimes worked these functions as a bartender, which meant that once again I had all the fun and he had all the work. However, sometimes we met interesting people and saw beautiful homes. We met some Cabots and Lodges and were amused by the various interactions and conversations.

One of the last Halloween parties at 93 Beacon, remembered as "the red dress party," was the largest. By this time both Clay and I did costumes. He had finally realized it was okay to let go, and when he saw me having so much fun, he decided to join in. Clay could always laugh at himself, he just needed to relax. Just before the party, David, an architect I worked with, and I did a booze run to New Hampshire. On the return trip there was a grand opening for a large Goodwill on Route 1. We stopped, and I found

Verne in the red dress   *Verne with the cockroach*

the "red dress with stole," and red Joan Crawford "come fuck me" pumps or CFMs. The store let me try on the pumps but not the dress. David held it up to me and we decided it would fit. Voila!

My life and Clay's was changed forever! Who could forget that vision of me in that dress! And I have pictures to prove it. Our friends Pat and Steve brought a friend of theirs that neither of us could stand, but they brought him every year anyway so we put up with him. Looking at the party album, I saw that he wore a cockroach costume. He had to put it on in the foyer and crawl up the grand staircase — all three floors — and into our apartment! Unforgettable! I have a picture of me in my red dress, CFMs, and blond wig sitting on his head. I think I farted there. If I didn't, I sure tried! This was the party that our landlord and his girlfriend (later wife) came to, with him dressed as a bricklayer and her dressed as a brick. No kidding. After she got him, their roles changed. His first wife had died years before and he had two grown kids. She assured him that she had no desire to raise little kids, but two years later they had two. No more parties for them!

The next party is one I've lived to regret many times over. It was meant to be a celebration of Clay's 50th birthday. He was working for Ellen. The story is still very hard to think about, let alone put in writing. I decided to throw a surprise birthday party for him and hired Ellen to cater it. I told Clay that I had made reservations at an expensive restaurant with a few friends. I prearranged with Ellen for her to tell Clay that she had an unexpected party come up and she needed him to cook for it. Looking back, I don't know why I did this; at the time, I thought it would be funny. I pretended to be very upset when Clay told me that he had to work. I told him that under no circumstance could he work the party — I had dinner reservations that I could not break. Clay insisted that he had to work the party and I pretended to be furious. I knew he would come flying through the front door, and that by the time he got back to our bedroom to change into his waiter's clothes, he would be half undressed. I had all of our guests crowd into the bedroom.

By the time Clay got there, he had his shoes, socks and shirt off and was unfastening his pants. Everybody hollered "Happy Birthday!" as he burst in. Looking very confused, he said to me "What am I going to tell Ellen?" I said, "Tell her to bring the food up!" Clay looked me straight in the face, and with no smile at all said, "You son-of-a-bitch, you mean I cooked my own birthday dinner?" I don't think anybody enjoyed that party. I know we didn't. I felt horrible; Clay felt that I had made a fool out of him and that was the one thing he could not abide. I don't tell this story very often... and I never told it in front of Clay. If I did, he would definitely leave the room! However, it is a measure of his character that he was quick to forgive — after about a day, all was forgotten and we moved on.

The last party at 93 Beacon was the 4th of July 1988. It was bittersweet, like the last one in Eau Claire. We knew we had to move very soon. Our rent had just gone up to $1800 per month; my work was drying up, and Clay didn't make a lot with Ellen.

By this time, the parties had gotten very large and expensive. At most of them, many of us were high on grass or some other drugs, but those were not allowed in our apartment. Our friends ranged in age from their mid twenties to one couple who was in their eighties and nineties! However, most were in their mid forties and fifties, and were settled married couples.

While many of our friends were now raising families, we raised parties. At one party, about half of us decided to enjoy fireworks from our roof so, with drinks and joints in hand, we climbed the ladder attached to the side of house and then climbed to the roof to watch the fireworks. By the time the fireworks were over, many of us realized that we were too drunk and too scared to climb down the ladder! We had to ask our neighbor (whom we didn't know) if we could come down through their apartment. It was very embarrassing and I'm sure that they were not happy to have a bunch of stoned partiers parading through their home! It's a good thing we were already planning to move!

Clay catering in Boston

CHAPTER NINE:
"INNOCENTS ABROAD"

Clay and I took many vacations over the years, some here in the States, some abroad, and some to more exotic locales. All were memorable for various reasons.

Our four trips to Europe were all fantastic. It was incredible to see all of these places that I had only read about and to experience different cultures. It was also eye-opening for us as a couple to get

Clay and Verne in Barcelona

Verne in Wales

Clay in Hawaii

Verne in Hawaii

to know each other as we traveled. You learn different things about your likes and dislikes when on the road. As I look back, several trips stand out — Luxembourg, because we witnessed the poignant site of women praying for their husbands and loved ones who were prisoners; Rome, because we lost our passports and money within hours of arriving but were rescued by the U.S. ambassador (this was thanks to my knowing a member of the Diplomatic Corps from my interior design contract). We also had an especially interesting journey down a mountainside in Costa Rica.

Luxembourg

It was the fall of 1971 and Clay and I had journeyed abroad with a copy of *Fodor's Europe on $5.00 a Day*, which we vowed to follow. We checked into a small hotel and crashed. When I awoke on Sunday morning to the sound of church bells ringing everywhere, I wanted to run outside to make sure I wasn't dreaming. Clay wanted to go to church, so we walked until we found a café near a small stone church. We had a latte and a croissant and enjoyed the peace. Before Clay went to Mass, we agreed to meet back there in about two hours and then we separated.

Luxembourg is medieval in feel and built on very hilly terrain that is criss-crossed with stone bridges and aqueducts. The aqueducts once carried the water for the whole country. From my vantage point in a small park overlooking the deep ravines, the view was breathtaking. The sun had a golden glow; the sky was very blue, and the bells from the many small churches made me feel that I was in a very pleasant dream. I started to walk, not knowing where I was headed. The old town seemed to consist of small parks, each with its own garden. Fall flowers were everywhere, although the tall, old trees had not yet started to turn. There were few people walking around, and those that were, seemed to be deep in their own morning thoughts. No one carried cups of coffee or tea like they do in the States and although there were small, intimate cafes along these stone walks, there were very few people in them. Luxembourg seemed to be a little country that thrived on quiet Sunday mornings, and where people lived a different life than I was used to.

I would walk for a while, then stop and look over a low stonewall and across a deep ravine. Below, there were small, winding streets lined with multi-colored houses. These had vivid, tiled roofs and small well-kept gardens tucked behind. Some had brightly-colored laundry hung on lines which blew gently in the cool morning breeze. No cars moved on the narrow streets; no music came from the opened windows; everything was serene and quiet, except for the ringing of the church bells. I walked for about an hour and a half, stopping once or twice to have a cup of coffee and a fresh breakfast muffin or to just sit and take it all in. I have never felt this content with myself and the world since that Sunday morning in Luxembourg.

Before long, it was time to go back and meet Clay so we could explore together. Clay was just coming out of the little chapel when I got back. We set out again, in a different direction. We soon came upon a long, yellow stucco building. It had many windows along the side and a small door. Outside the door was an oval mud track like a racetrack.

While we stood there, a small woman appeared a few feet from us. She appeared to be about 40 years old; she was dressed in a light green, longed-sleeved blouse, a long beige skirt and shoes that showed some wear but were well polished. Her complexion was dark and slightly lined, as if she worked outdoors in the sun. On her head, she wore a babushka of bright greens and browns tied under her chin; her hair was dark auburn with streaks of grey. There was no makeup that I could see.

In her hand she held a beautiful set of ruby-red rosary beads and she was praying. As we stood in the rich, golden sunshine, the door on the yellow building below opened. Men in some sort of uniform started to emerge. Suddenly a man came through the door; he looked up, gave a sad wave, and then joined the rest of the men who were walking around the mud track. I looked over to the woman and realized that she had tears running down her cheeks.

She seemed to be praying even harder; the tears were now flowing thick and fast, and she clutched the rosary to her bosom. Her rough hands moved continuously over the ruby red beads.

Clay and I realized that we were witnessing prisoners getting their morning exercise. The man she was watching was too old to be her son. Was he a lover, a husband, a brother? After about 20 minutes, the men started back through the door and as her man got to the door, he stopped, turned and waved. She waved back. I don't believe she had known we were there, but suddenly, she turned and saw us. She gave a faint smile, her eyes full of tears, and we smiled back through our tears. Then, she slowly turned and started up the hill as we turned and started down. We had just witnessed love, love at its deepest, and that memory stayed with us for the rest of our lives.

Costa Rica

Clay and I, and our good friend, Sandra, had the opportunity to visit our friend, Clark, who was assigned to the U.S. Embassy in San Juan, Costa Rica. Costa Rica is a beautiful Central American country, but it is not as developed as the United States. As a result, it offers a different experience for tourists.

The three of us decided to rent a car, travel to the west coast, and drive along the Pacific Ocean to enjoy the beaches and sample the food. We set out early in the morning on a fairly well-paved and well-traveled highway. We drove for a few hours and arrived at a seaside town named Jaco. We had a wonderful lunch and started down the coast towards Panama. After driving for about an hour, we decided to stop at a small hotel with a beautiful beach to do some swimming and have a nice quiet dinner. It was sheer heaven!

The next morning we had a hearty breakfast and continued along the coast, arriving at a delightful tourist town named Quepo, where we spent the day. After dinner, while Sandra and Clay took

"Vacation Fun"

*Clay and Clark
in Costa Rica*

*Verne and Clay
in Costa Rica*

Clay in Costa Rica

Verne in Costa Rica

Clay and Sandra at our last dinner in Costa Rica

a stroll, I studied the map and found what seemed to be a shorter route back to San Juan.

Instead of going back up the highway, we could take a road that cut diagonally toward San Juan, saving 69 miles and about three hours of driving time! As we left town, I stopped to get gas and told the attendant where we were headed, to which he replied "No go gringo."

I didn't tell the others what he said, and instead just headed up the paved road that started up the mountain. Clay was the first to notice and asked, "Why are you going this way? Isn't this the road the rental company said we shouldn't take because their insurance wouldn't cover us?" Sandra piped up, "Is this the pass Clark warned us not to take?" Being me, who always knows what is best, I said, "Don't worry about it, it's only 69 miles."

The road quickly went from being paved to gravel and got somewhat narrower. As we started up the mountain, I noticed that there was no guardrail on our right and that I couldn't see the bottom of the ravine. On our left, the mountain went straight up. We were on a very, very narrow, very, very curving road with no way to turn around. Oh well, I told myself, I have a sports car at home and I am a very good driver.

We traveled up and around for a few miles and then I realized that the only other vehicles on the road were 18-wheelers! Truck

Verne and Clay in San Juan, Puerto Rico

drivers down there have no rules and drive very fast, so this was not good.

After a few more miles, it started to get foggy and to drizzle. Then it got very foggy and started to rain hard. Conversation in the car had stopped and the moans started. As it grew darker and darker, I drove slower and slower, but the trucks didn't slow down. It got to the point where they came up behind me, layed on their horns, geared down and started to pass. As it got worse, I kept hearing in my head, "NO GO, GRINGO!" over and over. More trucks came up behind, hit their horns, geared down and passed.

Then there were trucks coming towards us, their high beams blinding me. My mind was racing; I was screaming in my head, "I CAN'T MOVE OVER! DON'T CUT IN YET! PLEASE GOD! OH GOD, PLEASE HELP ME! DON'T CUT IN YET! OH FUCK! SORRY GOD, I DIDN'T MEAN IT! WE'RE GOING TO DIE AND THEY ARE NEVER GOING TO FIND US! THERE WON'T BE ANYTHING TO SEND BACK! OH GOD! OH GOD!!!!!!!!!!!!!!!!!!!!!!"

The other thought running through my head was for our furry family at home, "WHAT ABOUT THE CATS? WHO'S GOING TO TAKE CARE OF THEM???????????????"

Suddenly, from somewhere in the car, someone said, "I have to go to the bathroom" followed by "Me too." I screamed, "I CAN'T PULL OVERRRRRRRRRRRR!!"

Finally, after what seemed a lifetime, I realized we had started down the mountain and that I could drive a little faster. The rain stopped; the fog lifted, and suddenly I could see lights below and stars above. I said to myself, "Thank you, God." Everybody gave a quiet sigh and a short laugh. I asked, "Does anybody need to go to the bathroom?" Both passengers replied, "Not anymore!"

Thus ended one of our more memorable trips!

"Dorchester"

Winter at Paisley Park

Our kitchen at Paisley Park

Clay at Paisley Park

Verne at Paisley Park

Barracuda & gold Mercedes

Gold Mercedes & blue Mercedes

Sailing with Sylvia in Boston

CHAPTER TEN:
DEEPEST, DARKEST DORCHESTER

That was the end of the good life as we knew it. We got some quality of life back, but it was so, so different. As I said, we had over 100 "friends" who partied with us twice a year in Boston. But, only about 20 or 25 stuck with us when we moved to deepest, darkest Dorchester. Our first apartment was in a not typical triple-decker, three-family home. It was on the second floor and was located near Fields Corner. It was two blocks from the T station and the train entered the tunnel under our house. Every time it did our house would shake, rattle and roll. We got used to it but our friends never did. Our dear friends, Marnie and Peter, had a friend who owned the house and the previous tenants had not left it in great shape. We made it livable, but Clay never forgot the smell. He said it smelled like poverty.

Once again, our whole life was changing. A lot of our good friends at this time were straight couples who had been together for many years like we had. Things were also pretty dire on the job front. It was clear that Clay needed to get out of catering. It was dragging him down healthwise and the long hours and job in general were making him very depressed. I was depressed as well. My work had all but dried up and I had totaled my beloved gold Mercedes. About this time, the University of Wisconsin's Eau Claire Audiology Department held their annual workshop in Boston. Clay went to several of the presentations. The last night that they were in town, we had them over for dinner. They offered to reinstate Clay back at the University and his tenure. At the same time, the head of the Interior Design Department at the University of Wisconsin/Stout had just died and there was a good chance I could be hired to replace him. After they left, we looked at each other and knew instantly, without saying anything, that we could not go back. The offers were tempting, but no way!

This was in the fall of 1989; and in the spring of 1990, I was hired by the GSA, a Federal agency, as an interior designer. The job offered decent money, so I took it. Clay enrolled in college for yet another degree. This degree landed him a job at Boston City Hospital as a counselor in their Methadone Clinic. We still partied, but with a little caution and a lot less money. We really knew who our friends were, and those who appreciated us and what we were offering, versus those who were just "hangers on."

My government job started out great. The first two years were wonderful. I met new friends and we introduced them to our established friends, but the overall pace of our lives was a lot slower. We were a lot poorer and perhaps a little wiser. We continued our European vacations and also made several remarkable tours to the West Coast to visit Glen. However, after those early years my job got progressively worse as I had trouble with my supervisors. I wasn't a "team player"— although I honestly had never pretended to be one! I did, however, take advantage of certain opportunities offered me by other agencies and thus had the opportunity to assist with projects for other clients, both in Boston and other New England locations.

Clay, on the other hand, was finally doing something that he loved. His work with those suffering from addiction allowed him to share that great gift of love and understanding that was so part of him. It was a gift he had been sharing with me and so many of our friends for decades. Now, he shared it with those who were in such great need.

We lived at three different locations in Dorchester and each was in a different parish. It turns out that you are identified by the

Our kitchen at
Park Street

locals by what parish you lived in. Our second location was Paisley
Park and it was a dream. It was almost as nice, in a very different
way, as 93 Beacon. Next came Moultrie Street which was Victorian
charm at its finest. We actually bought that house and it was a
wonderful investment. We sold it less than a year later and made
over $50,000 in profit.

Dining room at Christmas
at Paisley Park

Dining room at
Moultrie House

"Time Together"

Clay baking bread

*Verne and Clay going to
a wedding in 2010*

Verne's retirement

Clay in Alaska

*Verne and Clay going to
a wedding in 2015,
the last function they
enjoyed together*

CHAPTER ELEVEN:
PORTSMOUTH BY THE SEA

We discovered Portsmouth in 1981. I was working for an architectural firm in Brookline and their bread and butter account was Pease Air Force Base. Portsmouth still had that laid back small town feel and was a bit rough around the edges. Several inns in town had nice restaurants and there was one restaurant in town that rivaled the best in Boston. Oh God, The Inn At Petronella! Wonderful! The firm I worked for folded in 1982 so I approached Pease and they hired me as their design consultant.

Over the next few years, I developed a client base in Massachusetts, New Hampshire, Vermont and Maine and we dreamed of someday retiring to Portsmouth. On December 23, 1996 I noticed a small four-line ad in The Boston Globe. They were looking to hire a counselor with at least a master's degree to be director of volunteer services at AIDS Response Seacoast (ARS) in Portsmouth. The day after Christmas, Clay called about the job; we drove up for an interview that afternoon. By 5:00 in the afternoon, Clay had the job and we celebrated at The Library Restaurant. Here we go again!

Clay started work at ARS on January 2, 1997. It took us less than two months to realize that the reverse commute from Boston to Portsmouth was not going to work. I started researching homes in the area, and after putting in a 14-hour day, found a potential house online. It was a little pink colonial on Government Street in Kittery, Maine. I called the agent. Because the listing was in Maine, and I had called a realtor in New Hampshire, both realtors needed to be involved. I'm the type of guy that if I like what I see, and I know what it needs to make it work, I wanted to buy. However, Diane, our agent said she had some listings in Portsmouth that we should look at. We agreed to see what she had, and went back to Portsmouth and to 83/85 Gates Street. I wanted to buy both units as we had the money, but we settled on 85, a three-story Colonial within easy walking distance of the downtown and the waterfront.

On June 1st we moved in, sledge hammers in hand, although this time there was no party, just us. This was the beginning of our final journey together. After 18 years, we hoped one or both of us could end here. Most of our kids (cats) are buried here. Now I was the one commuting and Clay was walking to work. For awhile it worked. Clay liked his job and I could tolerate mine. But, eventually, we both bottomed out. I was backed into a corner in 2004 and forced to retire, as was Clay in 2002. City Hospital was more than happy to have him back and he was so happy to be back but that happiness was short-lived. By 2009, the 10-hour roundtrip commute was working against him as was his health and he had to hang it up. Oh, how he missed his clients and how they felt the loss. He never really got over having to give them up. He didn't want to let them go, as he felt responsible for helping them.

Not long after Clay died, I got a phone call on my cell phone which had the number Clay used before we both got cell phones. It was a man in great distress and he was crying. He said, "Gimme Clay! I need to talk to Clay!" Without thinking, I blurted out "Clay is dead." The man half moaned and half screamed and hung up. Realizing what I'd done, I tried to call him back, but he had been at a pay phone and I could not reach him. It just shows how great the need was and how special Clay was to these people. He knew how desperate they were and all he wanted to do was help each one.

When we arrived at our Gates Street home, we had five cats in jars and five "on the hoof" so to speak. We had decided that the five in jars were going to be with us 'till death do us part and that this was our final stop. It was high time to bury them. We dug a grave in the corner of the garden, near an old rock, emptied all the jars into a china bowl and I stirred the mix together. Thus, we buried our first family together.

Our life at Gates Street was much different than our life elsewhere had been, and the neighborhood was much different. I often wonder what our neighbors thought of us when we first arrived. What they saw was two middle-aged men (one being a gentleman) and five cats all arriving in a red Barracuda that, thank God, couldn't talk. At least most of our neighbors, both couples and non-couples, were about the same age and had similar tastes. For most, their party years were behind them just as ours were.

We did entertain at Gates Street, but no more large, loud bashes like those that marked our younger years; we had moved on to more quiet dinners with close family and friends. Life overall was slower, softer if you will. We enjoyed walking up to the square and spending time in coffee shops where we could read and talk for hours. We also liked sitting in the square and watching life go by. We had our favorite restaurants and both of us enjoyed getting involved with the community. Clay attended St. John's, where he sang in the choir and I got involved with The Common Table. The Common Table was a free community lunch that was put on every Thursday. People from all walks of life came, including the homeless and those with disabilities or suffering from addiction. Local chefs and volunteers served and prepared the food.

Clay showing off a painting at Prescott Park in Portsmouth

Ironically, it was thanks to my work with The Common Table that I put on one of my more memorable performances, but this time, it was for a good cause!

Honey Bun!

The Common Table is not a soup kitchen, as the meals we serve are prepared by a group of professional chefs who generously donate their time. They take turns cooking, and volunteers help with all of the prep, cleanup and serving.

Every June, our group put on a fundraiser called "The Uncommon Table," which is a big hit. It's a three-course dinner with wine, followed by entertainment, and an auction. Tickets were sold and as much as $30,000 could be raised. It was our main source of revenue. Auction items range from restaurant gift certificates to a week at a house in Ireland. As you can guess, the event was well-attended and was a big deal. Thus, it was something of a surprise that I found myself involved not once, but twice, with the entertainment.

The couple who started The Common Table are Judy and Lou Roberts. Judy is a retired dancer, so she headed up the entertainment. Every year, a theme was developed for the event and then the function hall, tables and entire night's program are built around that theme.

For many years, I was in charge of the hall design and also designed the décor for some of the tables. A few years ago, I was invited to be in the show along with several other fellows. I agreed, as I'm usually game for anything. That year wasn't so bad as we simply dressed up in plaid shirts, jeans and miners' hats and lip synched to "Sixteen Tons."

I guess we were well received because the next year, Judy asked me and Chuck, a fellow volunteer, to perform again. Unaware of what was in store, we agreed. The theme for this event was Broadway Musicals and we were to dance and lip synch to the

Honey Bun!

famous song, "Honey Bun," from South Pacific. This probably would have been funny enough, but when we discovered what our costumes would be, we both nearly had a breakdown.

Neither Chuck nor I are what you would call "muscle men." Neither of us have been to the gym in many years so our physiques are hardly finely sculpted works of art. Just dancing on stage was pushing the envelope. We had been innocently rehearsing the number, and having a lot of laughs, when we learned what Judy wanted us to wear.

The week before the dinner, we were presented with our costumes — or what little of them there was. We were each to don a coconut brassiere, a very short grass skirt, a blonde wig, and a flower lei, and wear nothing on our feet. The one good thing I can say about dress rehearsal is that no one was present except Chuck's wife, Sara. When we came on stage, Sara almost fell out of her chair!

As we sang the lyrics, Judy had concocted a whole dance routine. "My doll is as dainty as a sparrow; her figure is something to applaud; where she's narrow she's narrow as an arrow, and she's broad where a broad should be broad!"

As we mimed these words, we swung our hips and ran our hands seductively down our sides; then, we put our hands on our waists and wiggled our hips. Finally, we turned our backs to the audiences and "shook our moneymakers" once again.

These antics had Chuck and I laughing so hard that Judy made us start again. We could never get through more than one verse without breaking up. We also had to bump butts and do all kinds of other things. All this time, Sara was laughing so hysterically that Judy lost it herself and collapsed in laughter. I don't know how many times we stopped and started. "We'll never get through this without cracking up," I said, but Judy had us persevere.

At the next night's rehearsal, we finally did the whole number without losing it, but Sara and Judy were no help. Sara would start to giggle, then laugh, then everything would fall apart.

Finally, the big night arrived. The dinner was wonderful; the auction was very successful, and the entertainment started. Chuck and I were the last to go on stage. When we entered, the audience gasped, then giggled, then burst out laughing. Soon there were 200 people engulfed by one big belly laugh. We received a standing ovation, but no calls for an encore!

Clay had been working in the kitchen during most of the show. When I went on stage, he had come out into the audience. He had (mercifully) not seen any of the rehearsals so had no idea what to expect. The sight of me in a coconut bra and swinging my hips in a grass skirt was almost too much — he spent most of the number with his head in his hands. Afterwards, he rushed up on stage, gave me a big hug, and said, "Do you know how much I love you, Verne?" He admitted that he could never have done a number like that but he loved it that I would. I made him laugh and he always appreciated my zest for life, while I basked in his support.

The show made more money that year than any previous year. I'm pretty sure it was to ensure that no one had to sit through Honey Bun again!

"Believe me sonny! She's a cookie who can cook you 'till you're done!

Ain't bein' funny! Sonny, put your money on my Honey Bunny!"

Looking back on the 20 years we had together in Portsmouth, I recall what a rich life we had and I have no regrets. Portsmouth was very good to us. I think Portsmouth was where we finally came fully into step with one another. Close as we always were, we were not always in synch. Clay had wanted to move to Eau Claire while I wanted to remain in Columbus. I wanted to leave Eau Claire but Clay liked the academic life and wanted to stay. We compromised with the move to Boston, which I loved, but Clay found that time unsettling due to my self-destructive habits. Dorchester was a move we were forced to make and while we had some good times there, neither of us was truly happy there. Portsmouth was a place that we both wanted to move to, and it was here that we finally felt settled and at home.

*Verne's
50th birthday party*

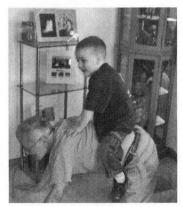

*Clay with Robert's
grandson*

Clay after
Mass General Hospital episode

CHAPTER TWELVE:
OUR LAST YEARS TOGETHER

It's time now to talk about our last few years together. This is the hardest thing that I've ever had to do and I hope that I'll never have to do anything like it again. I think Clay and I both started to realize that I would probably outlive him around 2010. It was getting harder and harder for him to get around because of his arthritis. He was given a dose of steroids and that helped him cope with his disabilities, but he was told that for safety's sake, he could have only two more treatments — any additional would eventually kill him. In 2012, Clay made the decision to continue with the treatments and take his chances. He also decided that, no matter how much he loved his job at the hospital, the commute was exacerbating his health issues.

At fist, we could still walk down to Market Square to sit and read but the walk took much longer and we had to stop frequently so that he could rest. Then, the week before our 44th anniversary on May 15, 2014, Clay became very confused. We made appointments with his doctors and I had to take him to the emergency room three times. The last time, they said that there wasn't anything wrong with Clay and advised him to see a drug counselor! I was furious!

For three nights in a row, Clay crawled up the stairs to my room and kept saying, "I wanna, I wanna" and "Please gimme, please gimme" over and over. I had no idea what to do. I put him in bed next to me and held him until he went to sleep. On the third morning, I went down to fix Clay's tea and Sylvia called from work to see how he was doing. (Sylvia was a nurse; we had become friendly with her when I did some interior design work for her first husband.) I told her that we were both very scared and she said she would call back when she got off work. I spent the day in bed with Clay, for it was only when I held him that he seemed to calm down.

At 3:30 that afternoon, Sylvia called back; she could hear Clay moaning in my arms. She told me to get him to the emergency room right away and to get Sharon, our friend and next door neighbor, to drive us. She would come up as soon as she could. While Sharon and I were waiting for the ER doctor to come in, Clay fell asleep and seemed calm. I told Sharon that they'd probably send him home again. But, when Clay woke, he was in very bad shape and it took three nurses to hold him down. They admitted him to the hospital and for the next two days he had to have someone with him all the time. The hospital could not provide this service, so neighbors helped me care for Clay.

On the third day, I was told that they did not know what was wrong and were transferring him to Massachusetts General Hospital in Boston. As they were putting Clay in the ambulance, he looked at me with tears in his eyes and said, "I love you Verne so much, gimme hug." When I got to the hospital, one of the nurses asked how long we had been together. It struck me then that it was May 15th, our 44th anniversary.

The next three and a half weeks are a blur in my brain. When I got to the hospital, fighting Friday traffic all the way, Clay was in a room with a very loud man from China and his wife. The noise was greatly disturbing to Clay. Sylvia was at the nurses' station, requesting a different room. Every time the man yelled for his wife, Clay jumped. Sylvia was finally successful in getting Clay a large single room. When I came back at 6:00 a.m., there were 15 different doctors in his room discussing his symptoms. They had put his arms and legs in a harness to keep him from thrashing.

Sylvia and her partner, Harry, were leaving on an extended vacation so I was able to stay at her house in Brookline,

Massachusetts and be near the hospital and Clay. Our Portsmouth neighbors took care of our animals. I spent my days sitting with Clay and they let me unbind him as long as I was in the room. Twice he managed to pull out the IV and feeding tube. His sister, Kate, and niece, Katie, came up from Tennessee, and my sister, Tippy, came from West Virginia. We all stayed at Sylvia's to be close to Clay. The hospital ran every test in the book but never got a firm diagnoses. They called it P.R.I.S — I no longer recall what the acronym stands for.

One doctor told me, while standing next to Clay's bed, that if he came out of it at all, he would have only about 25 percent brain function left. I called him out of the room and told him I never wanted to see him attending Clay again. I could tell by Clay's reaction, that he had heard him. On the third day, I came in and found that they had put Clay back in the room with the screaming Chinese man and this time there was no Sylvia around to fight for us. I went to the nurse's station and told them that if they did not get Clay another room, I was going to move him into the hallway. I guess I made an impression because they did find him a private room.

Tippy stayed with me for about six days but Kate and Katie could only stay for four days. While Tippy was here, I went home to get some paperwork and she joined me. I asked her if she felt I should discontinue all treatment — "pull the plug" as it were. She told me I had to ask Clay, so the next morning, I did. Clay replied with a great big "NO." After that, little by little, we began to see signs of hope. Clay was moved into a double room and over the next three weeks had a series of roommates. I noticed that he was starting to interact with them a bit and was encouraged. Then, one morning as I came down the hall to go to his room, I saw nurses walking a little man back into the room. "Another new roommate," I thought. When I entered, I realized it was Clay! They had him up and walking. The next morning, he was sitting in a chair, reading his Kindle. He gave me the biggest smile and hug and I knew then that he was going to be alright. I would have my Clay awhile longer.

After three more days, Clay was transferred to a rehab center in Portsmouth. I was told that he would be there for another four weeks. He had lost a lot of weight and was very weak. Four days later, he was home and cooking dinner in our kitchen!

I soon learned that Sylvia had promised to take Clay any where he wanted to go when he was well enough. He had chosen Quebec City.

Clay had come home from rehab in July, and by September, was up to taking a trip. We journeyed to Quebec and celebrated my and Sylvia's birthdays there. What a wonderful, glorious trip that was! Clay managed to walk up all 350 steps from the Old Town to the fort high above. I have pictures of us looking down to the St. Lawrence River and watching the ships come in. Clay smiled a lot on that trip. I can still see him and Sylvia coming out of the gift shop at the fort laughing at something. Sylvia treated him to a spoon holder marked "Quebec City" and he was touched by that.

During this time, Clay was still trying to enjoy as many of his favorite things as possible, even though he was well aware of his physical limitations. I believe that he was also aware that time was short. I've included a letter he wrote to an old friend; it's a good example of his sense of humor, gentleness and bravery in the face of serious illness.

Clay at Quebec Falls

Sylvia, Clay, and Verne in Quebec

"My dearest friend! How lovely to hear from you. I'm sorry that I didn't respond sooner, but I didn't know that you had sent me a message. I keep getting messages promising to take me back to my angst-ridden, lovelorn high school years (ghastly thought!) all for a fee, of course. But I digress.

As I say, it is a delight to hear from you – even though the news doesn't seem all that cheerful. I take it that you are single again. This is very sad. Experience has taught me that a college town is not a good place to age in, since it tends to abound with middle-aged complacency and underlines a sense of isolation. I have come to the opinion that old age sucks.

Go east young man! Portsmouth, for instance, is a very nice place to live.

Life here is good.

Verne and I have settled into a comfortable pattern after 44 years; each has given up any attempt to transmogrify the other into our idea of how another should behave; even if we know that our plan is really the best one — an old counseling theory, I know.

Verne is much the same, drinking more than I think he should (see above). He remains healthy as a horse. I on the contrary have encountered a few health issues, — rheumatoid arthritis, back surgery (twice), seizures, gall bladder removal, shingles, and an angioplasty cum stent, and severe cognitive issues — i.e., I can no longer type or spell, although I never could spell, for that matter. It is taking me forever to type this. I continue to sing in the church choir, even though I no longer have a voice and have trouble finding my place in the music. In fact, I recently fumbled for the right page, only to finally realize that I had the music upside-down! The other members help me to find the right page and point me in the right direction ("No Clayton, into the church, not out the door,"), so I get along. In fact, I find that if you stand there like a befuddled sheep, someone will herd you. — Clay"

Although both Clay and I had our fears and worries, we kept them tamped down and decided to live life as fully as possible while we could. Thanksgiving was wonderful, with Clay hosting our get-together the Sunday after, just as he had the last 44 years.

Christmas was soon upon us and I think we both realized it might be our last. We opted to not have gifts, but just enjoyed a nice tree, flowers and of course, a good dinner. We turned the page to the New Year and celebrated our 45th anniversary. We spent it with friends, but it was not fun. There was a poignancy to it, a sadness. When I look at photos of that day, I can see it in our eyes. Clay's did not have the twinkle that they usually did — I think he sensed that our time together was winding down.

On June 28th, we attended a concert with Sharon and Jan and during intermission Clay said he was having chest pain and needed to go to the emergency room in York. They decided to keep him overnight because they spotted something on his lung and wanted to do a biopsy the next morning, followed by an MRI. I stayed because he wanted me with him. Then they wanted to keep Clay another night because they said that they did not get enough tissue the first time, but he balked. He said, "Don't let them Verne; it hurts so much," so I brought Clay home. Clay kept refusing to call and get the results and much later on, I learned why.

After this episode, Clay seemed to shut down. He quit cooking, ironing (a chore he enjoyed), coming outside to sit with me, and eventually, even talking. I felt like he crawled into himself.

He cancelled all of his doctor and dentist appointments. On Saturday, August 25th, he became very sick and confused. I took him to the ER at Portsmouth Hospital where we were told that he had brain cancer. They planned to do an MRI in the morning. Clay had evidently known this for some time, which why he withdrew, but he could not bear to tell me. Now, with the diagnosis out in the open, he looked at me with that little smile on his face and said "Maybe it's time to pull the plug now, my love." The doctors wanted to start chemotherapy and I said "No way," but we did agree to start radiation.

We took Clay for his first treatment the end of July, but the radiologist felt he was too weak to endure it. They explained that because he had multiple lesions on his brain they would need to create a mask. They could only treat one lesion at a time and they needed to block out the others while they focused on that one. Thus, he would have his first treatment on Monday. I took Clay to that treatment and on the way home he became very agitated and upset. The next day, we went for his second treatment but the doctor said he wanted another MRI before he gave Clay radiation. I said "No" and brought him home.

Clay later became very upset, confused and incoherent so I called an ambulance and had him taken to the York ER. It was clear that things were going down hill fast. Friends joined us at the hospital and we spent the day trying to get Clay booked into hospice and trying to get a marriage license. He very much wanted us to be married, but when I applied and I told them I was divorced, they said I had to produce my divorce degree. Thankfully, my son was back in Belle Vernon with his mother, which is where the divorce was granted. He found the document at city hall and overnighted it to me.

Clay's sister and niece arrived by the next day and joined me at hospice. We walked up to Clay's room together. As we entered, I heard his death rattle and the nurse said, "Verne, he's waiting on you." We all embraced and kissed Clay. He opened his eyes and looked each of us in the eye. Then he closed his eyes, smiled and died. I had just said, "Clay, I got the divorce decree. We're getting married in an hour! The clerk is coming with our marriage application." His sister looked at me and said, "You killed him!" and we all laughed. It may sound macabre, but that was the Wilcox sense of humor, and we knew that Clay would have appreciated the irony of it all.

While I regret that we never married, and especially that I could not make it happen before Clay died — knowing how much he wanted it — I am at peace with what transpired. No two people could have been more married than Clay and I were. We knew what we meant to each other. We spent nearly our whole lives together. We grew and changed but always accepted each other, and always loved each other.

At the start of our relationship, gays could not have married. In our later years, that was possible, but by then, we were so tightly bound together, that we truly did not think about it — it was not a priority. We knew that one was not going anywhere without the other. Until Clay's passing.

This time, he had gone somewhere I could not go, although I know we will meet again. Clay's smile as he passed tells me that he was content; he knew that he was deeply loved and he knew that I wanted to marry him, and that was enough.

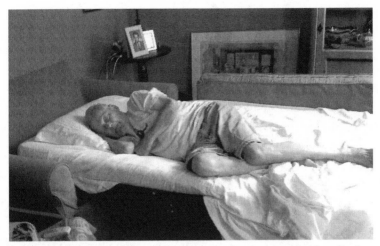

Clay sleeping on August 5, 2015, the day before he died.

Verne   *Clay*

CHAPTER THIRTEEN: GOING FORWARD… WITH LOVE

On August 6, 2015 at 9:30 a.m., my life as I'd known it ended. I found myself looking into a great void. I was relieved to know that I didn't have to watch Clay suffer any more. I was glad to no longer see his frustration when he dropped something or stumbled into something because he had lost his balance. I was grateful to no longer witness the slow destruction of this good and kind man I had loved for so long.

Still, Clay's passing did not really hit me until a group of us all went to Café Espresso for breakfast the morning of Clay's passing and the waitress asked, "Where's Clay?" How could he not be there? Clay had been by my side for more than 40 years—most of my life—how could I wake up and go on and he not be there?

Guilt was also quick to set in because one of my first thoughts was, "Thank you, Clay. I'll get the insurance money." It was something that we joked about but had really never talked about — even though it was always in the back of our minds. I felt guilt about a lot of things that first year — just being here, having the house, getting to live life.

It wasn't until June 16, 2016 that I started to keep a journal. The next year, on June 27th, I started to write this book. I knew then that I was starting to heal with Clay's help. Writing down the story of our time together, reliving all of the memories, good and bad, gave me purpose and allowed me to celebrate him and our journey. Thank you, Clay.

In February of 2017 two things happened that have had a great impact on my life. On the 10th, I had to put down dear Hoover, one of our cats. He had a stroke. I miss him dearly but letting him go was a kindness. Later that week, I went to the NHSPCA and found a grey and white tabby that I have named Sir Ashley Wilcox Stump. I can feel Clay's spirit is in him somewhere. Clay always said that if there was such a thing as reincarnation that he wanted to come back as one of my cats. Sir Ashley is constantly by my side. If I walk downtown, he follows. He loves Lucy and chases Henny.

The second thing was that I started doing AirBNB. I had moved my bedroom down to Clay's room and wasn't using the third floor. I think launching AirBNB has been my smartest move so far. I've met so many nice people from all over the world which has kept me from being so lonely. It also brought in $16,800 to the coffers which has been a big help — Clay would be proud! And, everybody loves Lucy and Sir Ash.

In the cooler months, I often sit in our front parlor by the fireplace, drinking a glass of champagne with our cats and my Siamese fighting fish close by. I still enjoy the holidays, but they are different. The small, traditional dinners in front of Sharon's wonderful old fireplace are no more, but old traditions die hard for me. This Christmas, I bought a small ham, potatoes, lima beans and corn to make succotash, and baked two pumpkin pies. The holidays are hard, but I'm still having our Christmas morning, just as Clay and I did for 45 years. The only thing missing is the bacon, eggs, toast and Clay.

I like to sit in the parlor; it's been my favorite room for 20 years because every item here has meaning. After Clay died, I had it painted a very deep red — walls and ceiling. On bright sunny mornings, the room is filled with warm, bright light. This room is so full of memories thanks in part to the decor. There's the take-off of a Hogarth that we bought from Anders Shafer one

Christmas while in Eau Claire. Below the painting is the wonderful cherry cabinet with mother of pearl inlays that was part of the Chinese exhibit at Lazarus. We bought it when the exhibit closed. I think we have Nixon to thank for that! On top of the cabinet there is a photo of Clay and I with "The Wahl," given to us for Christmas 1988 by our friends Tom and Sue. There is also a picture of Pop-Pop, my grandfather, a silhouette of my hero, President Lincoln — he's someone I've admired tremendously since I was a boy. There is a photo of Clay at age 24 (What a hunk!), and a vase of dried flowers from Clay's front garden that he picked six years ago.

Next to Anders' painting are the three small silhouettes that Clay gave me over the years. Near that same wall is one of the two miniature Christmas trees I put up this year. It was decorated with red balls and our pregnant pussy. I couldn't find a tree stand small enough so I stuck it in one of our tall glass vases. Kind of piss elegant, but that's me. The tree is on that old Jenny Lind table that we rescued from a junk shop and I restored.

On the other side of the cabinet, and in front of the other window is Mom-Moms' cherry plant stand, and on that is the brass container with the wandering iris that Sylvia gave us. The window treatments in these two windows are the frosted glass transom windows from our living and dinning room windows back in Eau Claire; we removed them and brought them East. I'm so glad we took them because the Eau Claire house has since been trashed.

One of our most cherished pieces is the Federal secretary that we bought on our first trip back to Columbus from Eau Claire. We bought it at Judy Stillwagon's antique shop. The secretary had been painted white and we assumed it was pine underneath, but when I stripped it down, I discovered it was a very fine rosewood veneer. It has always been one of our prized possessions and home to the pregnant pussy when she's not on a tree.

However, this room is also full of memories of us and our friends. There is not an item here that does not have meaning or that I don't know the history of; everything is special. It warms my heart to be among these things. Since Clay died, I've weeded out items throughout the house, and my house now feels even more comforting. Every item matters, whether it's Clay's copper cooking items, or all the miniature sports cars he bought me. They all have stories and take me back to times that are meaningful.

Clay — there are still a few things I must tell you. There are a few moments I would love to have just one more time. One of them is you walking up behind me, putting your arms around me, kissing me on top of my head and saying "Verne, you'll never know how much I love you." Another is you driving up in front of the house after church on Sunday in your blue car that matched your beautiful hair (Yes, that's right — Clay's hair was so white it had a bluish tinge!). You would sit in the car for a few minutes listening to something on the radio because you knew the noise bothered me and you didn't want to disturb me. You were always so kind that way.

I still write to you in my journal — usually when I'm having lunch with a Cosmo in hand. Nikkie and the gang at 5 Thai are like a family to me and they remember you and talk about you often. My journal is still on parchment paper and I write in ink. I carry it with me all the time. I try not to write on Sundays as that is the loneliest day of the week.

Clay, in closing, I would say that we were a successful couple, We shared many more laughs than tears, had many more fun vacations than not, had many, many more good meals than bad (I never cooked unless forced and that was a good thing!) and had many friends. We loved deeply, as only a few get to do. We were blessed. Farewell for now, Clay. As I once said to you, "When you want me to join you, just pull over and turn out your lights and I'll catch up." Love, Verne

Photo by Memories Studio

Verne holding Sir Ashley Wilcox Stump

EPILOGUE:

In closing our story, dear Clayton, I must relate the most amazing event that occurred this past Christmas of 2018. I was lying in bed on Christmas morning, sick with a heavy cold. I also felt sick emotionally. I felt so alone and afraid and ill that I could not even get out of bed to feed our animals.

Early afternoon came, and I was laying on my side, facing our door, when I felt someone standing beside our bed and behind me. I rolled over, looked up, and you were standing there. I said, "You're back!" and you reached down, and with the back of your hand, rubbed my forehead as you have done so many times before. You said, "You're okay, Verne!" I reached out for your hand, but you were gone. I know it wasn't a dream. You WERE there, and I know that you will always be there when I need you.

So, I say again, when you are ready for me, pull over and cut the lights. I'll be there, but I want you to spread your arms wide to catch me because I'll be kicking high and swinging that big, red purse! You'll never know how much I love you Clay!

— Your Verne

ABOUT VERNE STUMP

Photo by Memories Studio

Verne is a former interior designer whose work has been featured in major industrial, government and corporate buildings across the country. He is also an accomplished artist and seasoned traveler.

Originally from the Mid-West, Verne and his long-time partner, Clay, chose Portsmouth as their retirement city. Both became active in the community.

Today, Verne is pursuing a writing career, running an AirBNB, and keeping his three cats out of mischief.

Made in the USA
San Bernardino,
CA